CORRUPT

CORRUPT

The Inside Story of Biden's Dark Money

DICK MORRIS

Humanix Books
www.humanixbooks.com

Humanix Books
CORRUPT by Dick Morris
Copyright © 2023 by Humanix Books

Humanix Books, P.O. Box 20989, West Palm Beach, FL 33416, USA
www.humanixbooks.com | info@humanixbooks.com

Humanix Books is a division of Humanix Publishing, LLC. Its trademark, consisting of the words "Humanix Books," is registered in the United States Patent and Trademark Office and in other countries

ISBN: 978-163006-278-1 (Paperback)
ISBN: 978-163006-279-8 (E-book)

To President Donald J. Trump, a profile in courage

Contents

Contents

Contents

PART 3.   HOW CHINA GOT ITS MONEY'S WORTH FROM THE BIDENS

Contents

Contents

Contents

Foreword

By Peter Navarro

FROM RICHARD NIXON, HENRY Kissinger, and H. W. Bush to William Cohen, Bill Clinton, Haley Barbour, John Boehner, Mitch McConnell, and many more, the Chinese Communist Party (CCP) has skillfully used a variety of money pots, honeypots, flattery, and endless negotiations to seduce American politicians and thereby have its way with them. Yet across this infamous history—and this slender volume contributes mightily to that history—the seduction of President Joe Biden and much of his family must rank as the CCP's most successful and insidious.

Within these incendiary pages, Dick Morris, America's reigning dean of political strategy and tactics, completely unmasks the treasonous behavior of arguably the worst first family to ever darken the doors of the White House.

This book is so powerful that Biden may well attack Dick Morris for interference in the 2024 presidential race. After all, anyone who reads this book—including even Joe Biden's most zealous Democrat supporters—cannot in good conscience vote for a Judas who has sold our country down the Yangtze River for what, in the scheme of things, is only a relatively few pieces of silver.

If such an attack, Morris's defense would simply be that everything he reveals is the whole truth and nothing but the truth. In laying bare this whole truth, Dick Morris does not break any new ground in the fact department—all the various pieces of the Biden betrayal are part of the public record, as Morris's extensive research documents.

Instead, Dick Morris gives us something far more valuable than mere journalism. He leverages his chess grandmaster command of America's political arts to supremely and subtly interpret the political strategy and tactics of what has hitherto been a largely inscrutable communist China as it has operated in the American political arena and often on American soil.

Within these pages, both Joe Biden and communist China are revealed to be extreme dangers to an American nation now threatened from within by a variety of cultural, social, and economic crises largely of Biden's making and threatened from without by an authoritarian and fascist regime now engaged in the most rapid military buildup since World War II—even as this communist Chinese regime aligns itself ever more closely with America's other major existential threats in Russia, Iran, and North Korea.

What more can I say? Without further ado, I give you Dick Morris. Read, pray, vote.

Author's Note

EACH DAY BRINGS SHOCKING new allegations of the depth and breadth of the corruption of the Biden family. From China to Ukraine to Moscow to Iraq to Kazakhstan to Costa Rica to Florida to Romania and stops in between, the Biden family has been enriching itself by trading off the public offices and power accumulated by its mastermind: Joe Biden.

As this book is written, each news cycle exposes more allegations of illegitimately acquired wealth. Each day, I find myself racing to update the manuscript to keep up with the latest allegations of corruption.

(That's one reason this work is published as an e-book. In the often unbearably long period between when the author puts down his pen and the reader can pick up the book, new developments—specifically new Biden scandals—make yesterday's manuscript obsolete. But with an e-book, one can try at least to keep up even with the dizzying pace of charges of Biden's misconduct.)

As the 2024 elections approach, President Biden's alleged corruption and that of his family are emerging as key issues.

But while the investigations and media reports home in on Biden's corruption and try to pin down how much he got from who and when, a key element is missing: even as we learn about the vast amount of money China gave Biden, we know little of what China got in return.

The other end of the Biden-China quid pro quo is usually disguised as public policy, unconnected to any payments the Bidens received.

This book is in three parts. In part 1, I do my best to keep up with the mounting proof of what Biden got from China. In part 2, I discuss the Bidens' world tour for financial gain. In part 3, I probe the other side of the equation: What did China get from Biden?

- Did the money the Bidens got from China play a role in the administration's passivity in the face of Beijing's refusal to cooperate in the investigation of the origin of the COVID-19 virus?
- Is Biden's failure to get China to curb its carbon emissions while the rest of the world must starve itself of energy part of a policy that may have its roots in the president's financial dependency on the mandarins in Beijing?
- Is the president's passivity while China leads a global assault on the dollar connected to Hunter Biden's relationship with his financial benefactor in China?

- As China steals American technology, company by company, why does Biden do nothing to stop Beijing from requiring US firms to give up their trade secrets as the price of admission to China? And why does he do so little to stop industrial espionage directed by Beijing?
- Why did Biden allow Meng Wanzhou's release from prison? She is the daughter of the founder of Huawei, the company that has led the way in converting 5G cell phones into instruments used to spy on private citizens to enforce compliance with Beijing's orders.
- As Biden pushes for solar batteries and electric cars, both totally dependent on rare earth minerals, why does he do so little to break China's virtual monopoly on these crucial chips on which our future depends?
- Why is Biden so unconcerned about how China is developing a global economic empire by getting corrupt governments in third-world countries to borrow funds for infrastructure through its heralded Belt and Road Initiative? When the third-world dictators borrow the money, pocketing it or sequestering it in their Swiss bank accounts, China is only too eager to seize rare earth mineral assets that had been posted as collateral for the loans.
- Why does Biden let China get away with violating its obligations under the World Trade Organization (WTO) by undervaluing its currency and subsidizing its exports? Why won't Biden retaliate? We can't prove that China's seeming hold over Biden is due to its largesse to his family, but it does raise questions.

Preface

The Roots of China's Bribery of American Presidents

CHINA: PROSPERITY BASED ON BRIBERY

THREE COUNTRIES IN THE post–World War II era—Germany, Japan, and China—made it from the bottom to near the top of the global economic pecking order, but each used a totally different strategy. Germany recovered after its total defeat in the war through the Marshall Plan and massive American aid. Facing the threat of Russian communism, the US felt a sense of urgency about restoring the German economy to its prewar heights. And American policymakers, mindful of how economic humiliation had fueled Hitler's rise, were determined to stop postwar Germany from following the same path.

Japan's path was different as it recovered from the war. Denied the staggering amount of American aid that lifted Germany and Europe, Japan pulled itself up by ingenious research and development. As the world moved ahead with electronics, Japan focused on the miniaturization of technology. Encouraged by America's open markets, Japan became an export juggernaut and vaulted its way to recovery.

But China grew by means of bribery. Spending almost nothing on research and development, it purloined advanced technology from the West, particularly the United States. And what it couldn't steal it paid for through bribes. Bribery became an art form in modern China. The Chinese saw it as their only way to pull even with—and, if possible, ahead of—the United States.

After centuries under increasingly insular, incompetent, and corrupt emperors, China was first exposed to the West as the twentieth century began. But it led to what the Chinese call "a century of humiliation." This great and proud people, who had invented gunpowder, were enfeebled and weak and fell under the West's total domination. China's history since 1900 has largely been defined by failed strategies to escape its unimaginable humiliation. First, China tried rebellion against its Western oppressors. When that was crushed, it tried democracy. But that failed too when the Japanese invaded, starting World War II. After the war, Mao Zedong's communists took power. Mao, desperate to upgrade the Chinese economy, tried a "great leap forward" and then a "cultural revolution" to modernize China, but these, too, ended in total failure, with between fifty and eighty million dead. Finally, under Deng Xiaoping, in the 1980s, China tried fundamental free-market reforms—a variant of capitalism. This worked, but there was still something missing. China needed access to American markets.

But the American markets had begun to close. Stung by the success of first Germany and then Japan in selling exports to the US, pushing hundreds of thousands of businesses into failure and millions into unemployment, the American people were not about to replicate the pattern by opening their markets wide to China. So at last, China hit upon the solution: pry open American markets by bribing its political leader at the time, Bill Clinton.

It was a tall task. Americans hated the communist regime in China. The Korean War, begun when the communists tried to conquer the Korean peninsula, had led to thirty-seven thousand American combat deaths as China threw millions of soldiers into its "human-wave attacks" against American lines.

The legacy of the Korean War was to make a rapprochement between the US and China a political impossibility. And Republicans, led by then vice president Richard Nixon, vilified Democratic president Harry Truman, asking, "Who lost China?"

The US cut off all diplomatic relations with China and wouldn't let the communist regime into the United Nations.

It took a Republican president to open American minds to accepting the Chinese communists—the former hard-line anti-communist Richard M. Nixon, elected into office in 1968.

MR. NIXON GOES TO CHINA

After twenty years of isolation, Chinese-US relations recovered from their deep freeze, a change catalyzed by the Vietnam War. The war began as a proxy conflict between North and South Vietnam, with China and Russia supporting the north and the US heavily invested in defending the south.

As the war dragged on, Richard Nixon, acting through his secretary of state, Henry Kissinger, decided to open relations with communist China. In 1972, Nixon visited Mao in Beijing and opened the door to a new relationship. Their initial hope was to drain Chinese support for North Vietnam and to fan the emerging diplomatic conflict between the two communist superpowers, Russia and China.

The US withdrew its veto of Chinese communist membership in the United Nations and switched China's permanent seat on the UN Security Council from the nationalists to Mao.

The impact on China of the American about-face was dramatic. But it was the prying open of American minds to accepting China's communist regime that was the greatest contribution to China's economic evolution.

But still, American markets remained largely closed to China. Enter Bill Clinton.

HOW CHINA PAID OFF BILL CLINTON TO GET INTO THE WORLD TRADE ORGANIZATION

Mr. Clinton Sends American Business to China

Taking their cue from Nixon's visit and Deng's promarket reforms, the American business community saw vast new opportunities in China.

America's diplomats and political leaders overlooked China's brutal suppression of its own people and convinced themselves that China really wanted to change. They virtually ignored the Tiananmen Square massacre, where the communist government killed ten thousand prodemocracy demonstrators in 1989. In his 2011 book, *Death by China: Confronting the Dragon—a Global Call to Action*, Peter Navarro explains, "In this view, all totalitarian China needed to become democratic China was time—and a hefty dose of economic prosperity. By becoming more affluent, the argument went, 'they' will become just like 'us'—that is, a civilized democracy that respects free speech, intellectual property, human rights, and the rules of free trade, and the sanctity of the ballot box."[1]

Nobody embraced this benign theory more than my old client, President Bill Clinton. He pushed a policy of "engagement" with China and battled hard to normalize trade with Beijing.

But China still needed access to the US market for its newly born capitalism to succeed. So China resorted to its time-honored strategy of bribing American presidents to get what it wanted.

This time, it focused its largess on President Clinton. And boy did Clinton need the money.

Mr. Clinton Takes a Bribe from China

When I worked as President Bill Clinton's chief campaign strategist, I pressed him to raise money for advertising, even though the 1996 election was still a year and a half away. He had lost both houses of Congress to the Republicans in 1994, and the new Speaker of the House at the time, Newt Gingrich, and the new Senate majority leader, Trent Lott, were calling the shots on Capitol Hill. Clinton needed to get back in the game.

I urged him to raise $30 million to advertise and explain to the American people an idea I called *triangulation* (take the best ideas of the Right and the Left and combine them at the apex of the triangle and discard the rest). In practical terms, for example, it would reform welfare to require recipients to work and impose time limits on how long they could stay on the dole but also fund childcare and job training to help welfare moms get back on their feet.

Clinton and Hillary liked the idea, but how could they raise the money?

I soon found out. They got it from China, just like the Bidens are accused of doing. When I attended White House fundraising events, Clinton often introduced me to various Asian men and women whom I did not know and had never met before. They seemed out of place among Bill's Arkansas buddies, and I wondered why they were there.

Among the guests was the Riady family, who controlled the Lippo Group, which managed property, health care, financial services, retail, and education services in Asia. With capital from the Singapore state investment funds, the Malaysian sovereign wealth fund, and other Asian donors, they were heavy hitters in Washington. The Lippo Group attended the Clinton fund raisers and ultimately donated millions to the president's reelection fund and to the Democratic National Committee.

James T. Riady, the Indonesian who served as the head of the Lippo Group, was indicted on campaign finance violations. The Lippo Group admitted to making millions of dollars of illegal donations to Clinton.

Riady hired John Huang, a California resident who was a onetime official at Lippo, to direct all political donations and then got him a job at the US Department of Commerce, where he raised $3.4 million from the Asian American community.

Since foreign nationals are not permitted to donate to US candidates, Lippo employees were given cash to hand to US campaign managers, sometimes in amounts as large as $20,000.

In 1998, House Republicans investigated the "China Plan" to funnel money to the Clintons and other American candidates from Chinese sources, mostly those closely connected to the PRC (People's Republic of China).

Ted Sioeng, for example, is one of the largest donors. His family and his business enterprises contributed $400,000 to the Democratic National Committee (DNC) in the 1996 election cycle, at least half of which was funded by transfers from overseas accounts.

One transaction that brought a lot of unwelcome attention came after Vice President Al Gore attended a fund raiser at a

Buddhist temple. The donations, which came to nearly half a million dollars, were cash, checks, or money orders from worshippers who belonged to a controversial messianic Buddhist sect called Sum Ching Hai.[2] It is obvious that the circuitous path the money followed was designed to cover up its Chinese government origins.

When I was in Little Rock working for Clinton, I often indulged my taste for Chinese food by eating at a local restaurant owned by Yah Lin "Charlie" Trie.

It turned out that Trie gave half a million dollars to the Presidential Legal Expense Fund established by the Clintons to defray the legal bills they incurred defending themselves against charges by federal special prosecutor Kenneth Starr.

The donations Trie rounded up were sufficiently suspicious enough that the Democratic National Committee hired private investigator, Terry Lenzner, to ferret out possible fraud. And boy was there fraud! It turned out that the majority of the funds were donated through money orders, some of which were consecutively numbered and many of which had misspellings, including "presidential" spelled as "presidencial." Some had been written in identical handwriting. Lenzner found that some of the "donors" were people of very modest means, making only $20,000 or $30,000 a year, and due to their low incomes, logic suggests these "donors" could not possibly have been the real source of the large donations attributed to them.[3]

Obviously, Trie was distributing funds he got from China or some other source to many donors who would then, in their own names, give the money to the Clintons in order not to run afoul of legal limits on how much individuals could each contribute.

When a congressional committee questioned me about the Clintons' reliance on funds from Asia, I quipped that I knew the ads I was writing cost a lot of money but that I had no idea the Clintons were sending out for Chinese food!

Mr. Clinton Delivers for China . . . *Big Time!*

China got what it paid for. Its investments in the Clintons' political careers, minor compared to the funds that flowed to the corrupt Biden family, bought China its entry into the global economy.

In the history of the United States, no president has ever compromised American national and economic interests more than Bill Clinton did in his dealings with China. As one who bears some personal responsibility for his political rise, I believe he could not have foreseen the catastrophic consequences of his actions. But the money trail of Chinese government support for his political career makes his denials untenable.

Clinton sold America on letting China into the global economic system without adequate checks and balances, saying that Beijing would not take unfair advantage of the opening Clinton afforded it.

When he was running for president in 1992, he roundly criticized George H. W. Bush for "coddling the butchers of Beijing"[4] after the Tiananmen Square massacre and promised to place strict conditions on China's annual most favored nation (MFN) trading status. But once in office, Clinton reversed course and granted permanent normal trade relations to China.

Before China got the MFN trade status with the United States in 2000, it did not pose nearly the economic or strategic challenge to America that it does today. China's trade surplus with the United States increased tenfold in the first eight years of its WTO membership! *Tenfold*! From $35 billion to $348 billion.

When he first let China into the WTO, Clinton dressed it up as a step that would be of great benefit to American workers. In his speech on March 9, 2000, as his second term was ending, he called it "a one-way street," where China would have to open its markets to our businesses. He even suggested that it would encourage China to play "by global rules." While he admitted that it "will not create a free society in China overnight" and he did not "guarantee that China will play by global rules," he said he believed that over time, "it will move China faster and further in the right direction."[5]

And don't worry that China might cheat. Clinton assured us, "We'll get valuable new safeguards against any surges of imports from China. We're already preparing for the largest enforcement effort ever given for a trade agreement."[6]

The dark reality of what happened when China walked through the door Clinton had graciously opened was well captured by future US trade representative Peter Navarro in *Death by China*, which he coauthored with Greg Autry.

Navarro writes in *Death by China* that Clinton's folly led China to begin its "full frontal assault" on America's factories, using what he called "weapons of job destruction" like illegal export subsidies and currency manipulation. Navarro says that China's policies led American corporate executives to realize that "by taking advantage of China's elaborate web of export subsidies, they could produce more cheaply on Chinese than on American soil and, if they did not, their competitors would." He sums up the conclusions of US business leaders as "If you can't beat China, join it."[7]

Navarro counters the explanations of expatriate American businessmen that they moved their companies to China to take advantage of its vast untapped market. He explains, "The most important propellant [for moving to China] was not access to its 1.3 billion consumers."[8] They were dirt poor and had little buying power. Rather, he says that moving to China helped American businesses evade the tough environmental and safety standards in the US and let them take advantage of China's export subsidies and unfair trade practices to sell to other countries from their new Chinese base, often right back to the very same United States from which they had just fled.[9]

The Chinese experiment in bribing Bill Clinton by giving him money for his advertising, campaigns, and even legal defense was one of the most successful in world history. Beijing discovered that the key to America's treasure was payoffs to its president.

It was a discovery that the corrupt Biden family would build on.

PART 1

THE EDUCATION OF JOE BIDEN IN THE WAYS OF THE WASHINGTON SWAMP

CHAPTER 1

UP FROM POVERTY

The Education of Joe Biden in the Ways of Washington

IN 2008, WHEN PRESIDENT Barack Obama tapped Senator Joseph R. Biden to be his vice presidential candidate, he was elevating to power the single poorest member of the US Senate. It was affirmative action at its best.

Joe Biden began his political career in relative poverty. For all his thirty-six years in the US Senate, Joe Biden had the distinction of being among the poorest of senators.

In 2009, as he left the Senate to become vice president, CBS News reported that his net worth stood at a paltry $27,012.[1]

Was he honest? You must believe he was—or was he just a totally inept criminal? His poverty was his badge of honor.

But neither his poverty nor his honor lasted as he left the Senate for the greener pastures of a high office in the executive branch.

As vice president (2009–17), Joe began to make money. His net worth rose to $2.5 million. A big increase, but not really evidence of corruption. That would come later.

His salary as vice president peaked at $250,000 per year. His pension from the US Senate also ran to about $250,000 per year,[2] and he published a memoir, *Promises to Keep: On Life and Politics*, while in office, so the increase in net worth was not astonishing.

But it was in the interval between the end of his vice presidency and the start of his presidency that Biden really hit it big, making $17 million ($11.1 million in 2017, his first year out of office; $4.6 million in 2018; $1 million in 2019; and, as he ran for president, $630,000 in 2020).

In 2023, as he prepares to run for reelection, his net worth is reportedly up to $8 million.[3]

It has not been a gradual assent but more of a get-rich-quick process that brought Biden to millionaire status.

Biden's income in 2017, his big year, is protected from public view by two S corporations[4] he established: CelticCapri and Giacoppa. He funneled most of his income, $10 million in 2017 and another $3.2 million in 2018, through these two S corporations.[5]

Since S corporations are not required to disclose the sources of their income, we are left to speculate on how Biden cashed in big time in 2017.

CHAPTER 2

THE MISSING $10 MILLION

HOW MUCH DID JOE Biden make from his and Hunter's dealings in the years between his vice presidency and the White House?

We don't know and likely never will, but we can get an idea by examining what is not in Joe Biden's tax returns. In 2017–18, the Bidens reported an income of $15.7 million to the IRS. Where did that much money come from?

Biden's main source of income was his book, *Promise Me, Dad: A Year of Hope, Hardship, and Purpose*, about his deceased son Beau. Per BookScan, the book has sold more than three hundred thousand copies, which would generate between $6 million and $9 million in total hardcover sales. Typically, publishers pay authors 15 percent of their total sales in royalties, which would give the Bidens between $900,000 and $1.3 million in royalties.

Add that to his other sources of income—$4 million in speaking fees, $540,000 from the Penn Biden Center for Diplomacy and Global Engagement, a reported $120,000 from social security, and $250,000 million from his pension—and it comes to, at most, $6.2 million, about $9 million to $10 million less than his reported income.[1]

As Senator Ted Cruz (R-TX) said on his podcast, *Verdict with Ted Cruz*, "You're looking at a tax return that has $10 million in cash that came from a mystery source."[2]

Where did the extra cash come from?

We don't know, but we can speculate.

The *New York Post* reports,

Joe's son Hunter has shouldered a fair share of responsibility for financing the family's lavish lifestyle, according to messages found on his laptop. . . . Hunter reportedly secured various business deals with Ukraine and China by allegedly trading on his father's position. In return, Biden was given a percentage of the profits, according to Hunter's former business partner, US Navy veteran Tony Bobulinski. . . . During the 2020 presidential campaign, Bobulinski revealed that Joe Biden, referred to as "the big guy" in messages on Hunter's laptop, received a cut of the proceeds from his son's overseas dealing. In one message, in January 2019, Hunter complains to daughter Naomi about kicking back half of his earnings from lucrative board positions and his own firm's legal work to support his father and stepmother.[3]

With the cash, Joe and Jill bought two homes in Delaware worth a combined $4 million and made investments totaling another $4 million.

How much more did the Biden family make from the corruption in China? The Ukraine? Romania? Kazakhstan? Costa Rica? Iraq? How much did they make from charter schools in Florida?

The Biden family business received over $20 million from Russia, Ukraine, and Kazakhstan *while* Joe Biden was in between jobs, having left the vice presidency and about to run for president, House Committee on Oversight and Accountability chair James Comer (R-KY) revealed. The committee previously unveiled two tranches of Biden business bank records. Those showed the Biden business received at least $10 million from business schemes in Romania and China.[4] In total, nine Biden family members received payments from the family foreign business ventures, including two of Joe Biden's grandchildren.[5] Comer predicted in June that the committee's work would ultimately show the Biden family accepted up to $30 million from its foreign business dealings.[6]

The committee found that "during Joe Biden's vice presidency, Hunter Biden sold him as 'the brand' to reap millions from oligarchs in Kazakhstan, Russia, and Ukraine," Comer said in a press release. "It appears no real services were provided other than access to the Biden network, including Joe Biden himself."[7]

Comer added, "It's clear Joe Biden knew about his son's business dealings and allowed himself to be 'the brand' sold to enrich the Biden family while he was Vice President of the United States."[8]

Comer said that in July,[9] the Biden family business caused six banks to flag more than 170 deposits of large amounts of money in suspicious activity reports (SARs) to the treasury for review, twenty more than previously known.[10] SARs "often contain evidence of potential criminal activities, such as money laundering and fraud," according to a 2020 Senate report.[11] Comer believes the Biden family opened more than twenty shell companies to hide payments and launder money.[12] "When you set up a bunch of shell companies for the sole purpose to launder money, that is called racketeering," he said.

The House Committee on Oversight and Accountability said that the "Biden family bank records show they, their business associates, and their companies received over $10 million from foreign nationals' companies."[13]

Most of the money was carefully and skillfully hidden from public view by what the committee described as "a complex money laundering scheme involving millions of dollars from foreign entities that investigators contend went to President Joe Biden and nearly a dozen members of his family."[14]

The committee staff examined thousands of bank records and legal documents depicting nearly two dozen limited liability corporations (LLCs) established by Biden family members to receive payments from private clients, corporations, and foreign governments, including China and Romania.

They found that the "Biden family members and business associates [had] created a web of over 20 companies—most were limited liability companies formed during Joe Biden's vice presidency."[15]

The breathtaking scope of Joe and Hunter Biden's alleged corruption in dealing with China and other countries came to light when the House Committee on Oversight and Accountability, chaired by James Comer (R-KY), released its findings on May 10, 2023.

The committee said, "The Bidens made millions from foreign nationals providing what seems to be no services other than access and influence."[16]

They also noted how hard the Biden family worked to conceal its corruption: "From the thousands of records we've obtained so far, we know the Biden family set up over a dozen companies when Joe Biden was vice president. The Bidens engaged in many intentionally complicated financial transactions to hide these payments and avoid scrutiny."[17]

How much of the money went directly to Joe Biden personally is a secret that the family made hard to unravel. The Comer committee noted, "The Biden family received incremental payments over time to different bank accounts. These complicated financial transactions appear to be meant to conceal the source of the funds and reduce the conspicuousness of the total amounts made into the Biden bank accounts."[18]

Charging the Biden family with "financial deception," the committee said that the Chinese Communist Party and Chinese intelligence "hid the source of the funds paid out to the Bidens by layering domestic limited liability companies. The Biden family and associates' activities in coordination with Chinese nationals and their corporate entities appear to be an attempt to engage in financial deception."

The committee wrote, "Multiple Biden family members received money from the Chinese after it passed through an associate's account. Additionally, Hunter Biden received money directly into his company's account from a Chinese-controlled entity."[19]

When Biden ran for president, he told the American people that he and his family had received no money from China.[20] But Hunter's partner, Devon Archer, revealed to Congress that while Biden was vice president, Hunter would "put his father on speakerphone at business dinners and in other situations, according to lawmakers present for the closed-door briefing."[21] Calling his father in front of a potential client was Hunter's way of showing how close he was to his father, with the clear implication that Joe's power and influence were for sale in a neat family collaboration between father and son.

The *Wall Street Journal* reported, "Archer testified that there were about 20 phone calls including Joe Biden. The calls took place while Joe Biden was vice president and included one during a dinner in Paris with a French energy company and another in China with Jonathan Li, the CEO of Chinese private-equity firm BHR."[22]

Comer said that Archer's testimony "confirms Joe Biden lied to the American people when he said he had no knowledge about his son's business dealings and was not involved."[23]

Hunter's legal counsel minimized the importance of the calls, saying that they did not concern the son's international business.

"It's well known that Hunter and his father speak daily," said lawyer Abbe Lowell. "What Mr. Archer confirmed today was that when those calls occurred during Hunter's business meetings, if there was any interaction between his father and his business associates, it was simply to exchange small talk."[24]

"In the more than twenty such calls" that involved the vice president, Archer recalled that "the Bidens never discussed business, keeping the conversation light, discussing the weather and gossip."[25]

Vice President Joe was apparently just a weatherman, advising his son when to wear a raincoat and galoshes.

But the Biden family created a web of more than twenty LLCs, during and after Biden's vice presidency.

These companies would receive large checks and wires from Chinese sources and then would distribute the proceeds in smaller payments to family members. The committee said, "These complicated and seemingly unnecessary financial transactions appear to be a concerted effort to conceal the source and total amount received from the foreign companies."[26]

An IRS whistleblower who came forward to testify confirmed claims by House Republicans that Hunter Biden and his companies raked in over $17 million from foreign sources over several years, beginning while his father was vice president.[27]

The House Committee on Oversight and Reform interviewed two IRS whistleblowers alleging political misconduct throughout the Hunter Biden investigation: Special Agent Joseph Ziegler, whose identity was revealed during the hearing, and his IRS supervisor Gary Shapley, who previously blew the whistle on alleged political influence surrounding prosecutorial decisions throughout the yearslong federal probe into the president's son.[28]

Ziegler told Chairman Comer that Hunter Biden, his family members, and his business associates received over $17 million due to business dealings in China, Ukraine, and Romania.

Those deals included multimillion-dollar payments to Biden family–linked companies from 2014 to 2019, including $7.3 million from Ukrainian energy company Burisma Holdings.

"This brings the total amount of foreign income streams received to approximately $17 million, correct?" Comer asked Ziegler.

"That is correct," Ziegler responded. "The purpose of documenting the foreign sources is part of a normal international tax investigation. . . . We have to figure out where the money is coming from."[29]

The interval between the vice presidency and his inauguration as the forty-sixth president was an odyssey of world travel in search of payoffs for the entire Biden family.

Like a seventeenth-century European monarch who betrothed his sons and daughters to foreign royal courts in search of alliances and dowries, Joe dispatched Hunter and his brothers Frank and James to faraway lands to use the family name to get large salaries, loans, and investments.

So come with me now to retrace the footsteps of Hunter and the rest of the corrupt family in search of fortune.

Part 2

JOE, HUNTER, AND THE REST OF THE BIDENS TOUR THE WORLD IN SEARCH OF MONEY

PART 2

CHAPTER 3

MR. BIDEN GOES TO BEIJING

ON DECEMBER 4, 2013, A year into his father's second term as vice president, Hunter walked down the gangplank of Air Force Two into the open arms of a Chinese delegation. The Beijing officials were not there primarily to meet him; they had come to see the vice president himself, who was on the flight. But for Hunter, this was the equivalent of entering the promised land of wealth, privilege, and fortune.

It was unusual for a vice president to bring his son to China, but the purpose of Hunter's inclusion in the traveling party soon became apparent to their hosts: Hunter was to be the back-channel conduit for the money China may have funneled to the vice president to foster their "relationship."

While aides carried the bags of the vice president's traveling party, it was Hunter who was the true "bag man," sent to negotiate deals in Joe Biden's wake.

Hunter was the ideal man for the job. His intimacy with his father was well known. Ever since his brother's death in 2015, Hunter was Joe's only surviving son. Everyone in the power circles in China, Ukraine, Moscow, and dozens of other countries knew that if you cut a deal with Hunter, you were at the same time cutting one with Joe.

And the goodies immediately started to flow soon after that meeting:

- Hunter brokered some $1 billion in loans and investments between the Bank of China, owned by the Chinese government, and businesses in China. Later, the deal grew to $1.5 billion, and as Schweizer reported in *Profiles in Corruption*, the bottom line grew to $2 billion by 2020.[1]
- The deal with the Bank of China brought Hunter a 10 percent equity stake in private-equity firm BHR in addition to other fees yet to be disclosed. He made tens of millions.
- Hunter got $3 million from CEFC, the Chinese energy company. Hunter had to share the money with the other members of the family. He paid one-third to Hallie Biden, his daughter-in-law and the widow of Beau Biden, Joe's deceased son. (Hallie did double duty in the Biden entourage, serving as both Beau's widow and Hunter's mistress for three years.)

By the time all the partnerships, commissions, fees, profit sharing, and direct payoffs were tallied up, Peter Schweizer makes clear that "the Biden family received some $31 million from

Chinese businessmen with very close ties to the highest levels of Chinese intelligence during and after Joe Biden tenure as vice-president."[2]

Hunter knew that he could be paid off and still be sheltered by American law. The US law requires the president and his wife to disclose their income and its sources, but it says nothing about his son. Hunter could fly well under the radar, protected from ethics checks imposed by Congress to insure against just the kind of corruption in which China and Hunter were about to engage.

JOE BIDEN'S ROLE: THE SMOKING GUN

As this book was entering its final stage of writing, a whistleblower, IRS Criminal Supervisory Special Agent Gary Shapley Jr., provided the House Committee on Oversight and Reform with a smoking gun by exposing how Joe and Hunter Biden played the game of influence peddling.

The evidence emerged because Hunter Biden was furious that his colleague Henry Zhao, a top-ranking Chinese Communist Party leader and CEO of Harvest Fund Management, a front for the Chinese government, appeared to be welching on a commitment to invest $15 million in Hunter's company, Burnham Financial Group.

In anger, Hunter sent this message to Zhao on WhatsApp: "I am sitting here with my father and we would like to understand why the commitment made has not been fulfilled. Tell the director that I would like to resolve this now before it gets out of hand, and now means tonight. . . . And, Z, if I get a call or text from anyone involved in this other than you, Zhang, or the chairman, I will make certain that between the man sitting next to me and every person he knows and my ability to forever hold a grudge that you will regret not following my direction. I am sitting here waiting for the call with my father."[3]

Court documents indicate that Hunter was partially successful in his bluster because Zhao's firm soon sent $5 million.[4]

Shapley and a second, unnamed IRS investigator also told the House Committee on Ways and Means that Joe Biden, as vice president, attended other business meetings with Hunter and his Chinese partners, belying his statement that he had no knowledge of Hunter's financial activities. Biden family friend and business partner Rob Walker told the FBI that he was present when Biden "stopped by a meeting at the Washington, D.C., Four Seasons hotel with executives from CEFC China Energy."[5]

The investigators also confirmed what many Republicans had suspected: In 2020, the FBI authenticated that a laptop containing damning data, pornographic images of sex and drug use, and business communications with Joe Biden, left with John Paul Mac Isaac, the owner of the Mac Shop, in 2019, belonged to Hunter. This was about a year before the rest of the country even knew it existed.[6] The discrediting of the laptop by fifty former intelligence agents who claimed it was a product of Russian disinformation has formed much of the basis for Donald Trump's claim that the 2020 election was rigged. Now that we know that the DOJ knew it was genuine, former president Trump's charge that we would never have elected Joe Biden had we known then what we know now about the Biden-China relationship must be taken more seriously.

Shapley also revealed that the FBI's national security division that investigates foreign spies "took an interest in Biden's dealings with China."

Shapley said that their interest was particularly focused on Hunter's "work with CEFC China Energy, which had links to Chinese military intelligence."[7]

Hunter got $6 million from CEFC, and he referred to one of his CEFC associates, Patrick Ho, as "the fucking spymaster of China" in a 2018 audio recording. Hunter was paid $1 million to represent Ho when he was charged with a multimillion-dollar scheme to bribe leaders from Chad and Uganda. Ho was convicted and sentenced to three years in prison.[8]

As Hunter agreed to a plea deal, Shapley revealed that federal prosecutors and IRS investigators had originally recommended felony tax evasion charges against Hunter Biden for the years 2014 to 2018. Shapley estimated that Hunter evaded $2.2 million in taxes.[9]

Perhaps more significant for the Biden administration is the massive evidence Shapley produced of interference in his investigation of the president's son by the Justice Department.

Shapely revealed the following:

- Biden-appointed prosecutors in Washington, DC, and California rejected the requests of David Weiss, US attorney for the District of Columbia, to charge Hunter with tax crimes. Shapely noted, "The denial prevented Weiss from taking aggressive steps in the investigation or from bringing charges against Biden in jurisdictions where he allegedly committed tax fraud."[10]

- FBI and IRS agents were blocked from searching Hunter's residence and a guesthouse at Joe's family compound, where Hunter frequently stayed. Shapley said his superiors rejected the request for a warrant because of the "optics" involved.[11]

- When the IRS sought to search Hunter's storage locker and when the FBI wanted to interview Hunter, Shapley says the DOJ tipped off Hunter.[12]

CHINA PUTS JOE BIDEN ON ITS PAYROLL

Joe Biden was also indirectly on the payroll of the Chinese government ever since his retirement as vice president in 2017 until his election as president in November 2020.

Out of a job, unemployed, and with no steady source of income, the former vice president cut a lucrative deal with the University of Pennsylvania to found the Penn Biden Center.

Part of Joe Biden's new wealth came from $775,000 he made over four years from the University of Pennsylvania (to lead the Penn Biden Center as the Benjamin Franklin Presidential Practice Professor). Most of the money came in anonymous donations to the center—fortune cookies, really—from various sources in China.

The Penn Biden Center is a peon to globalism. In its mission statement, it states that it is "founded on the principle that a democratic, open, secure, tolerant, and interconnected world benefits all Americans." It credits US global leadership with "enabling virtually every advantage we enjoy as Americans and helping to ensure our safety, our prosperity, and our way of life."[13]

What a lofty description of an enterprise whose main purpose was to funnel money to Joe Biden during his years in between public offices, from 2017 to 2021!

Biden was named the Benjamin Franklin Presidential Practice Professor at the University of Pennsylvania, a post that earned him a $372,000 salary in 2017. He stayed on for the next few years, earning $405,000 in 2018.[14]

What did he do for the money?

Not much. The *Philadelphia Inquirer* kindly describes his role as involving "no regular classes and around a dozen public appearances on campus, mostly in big, ticketed events."

But more worrisome is the source of the money paid to Biden.

Congressman James Comer describes how "the Penn Biden Center appears to have acted as a foreign-sponsored source of income for much of a Biden Administration in-waiting. Between 2017 and 2019, UPenn paid President Biden more than $900,000, and the university employed at least ten people at the Penn Biden Center who later became senior Biden administration officials."[15]

Comer's committee says, "UPenn received millions of dollars from anonymous Chinese sources, with a marked uptick in donations when then-former Vice President Biden was announced as leading the Penn Biden Center initiative."[16] Donations from China to the Penn Biden Center tripled and continued while Biden was exploring a run for president in 2019–20.

The Penn Biden Center's generosity to Joe Biden and its connections to China attracted the attention of Paul Moore, the former chief investigator for the Department of Education. Moore commented on a "startling" spike in Chinese donations to the University of Pennsylvania after President Joe Biden opened his think tank at the school in 2017.

Moore called the increase in Chinese support for the University of Pennsylvania "extraordinary, noting that the University received over $100 million from China-based contributors between 2017 and 2022, compared to only $19 million in the four years before 2017."[17]

The National Legal and Policy Center (NLPC) filed a complaint with the US Department of Education demanding that the university disclose the identity of the anonymous donor(s) of $22 million since 2017, including $14.5 million given on May 29, 2018, shortly after the opening of the Penn Biden Center. The NLPC says, "Altogether, China gave $67 million in two years to the University of Pennsylvania."[18]

One of the more prominent future Biden administration officials to find lucrative employment at the Penn Biden Center was future secretary of state Tony Blinken, who served as the center's managing director.

The Penn Biden Center conduit for funneling money to Joe Biden came into full public view when classified government documents were found at the center, an echo of the archive scandal that hit Donald Trump. Comer's committee said, "It is imperative to understand whether any Biden family members or associates gained access to the classified documents while stored at the Penn Biden Center."[19]

After all, there was nobody at Mar-a-Lago, where the Trump documents were stored, but the Penn Biden Center, where Joe's documents were located, was funded by the Chinese Communist Party, and CCP officials may have been curious about what documents were lying around there.

The exact amount of Chinese largesse to the Penn Biden Center—and to Joe personally—remains a tightly guarded secret at the university, a confidentiality perhaps reinforced by President Biden's decision in 2021 to appoint the president of the University of Pennsylvania, Amy Gutmann, to serve as ambassador to Germany.

Joe and Jill Biden earned $22 million during his years out of office from 2017 to 2021. So the close to $1 million he got through the University of Pennsylvania was not an insignificant share of his income. To that extent, we seem to have elected a president who was, in effect, on the payroll of our nation's biggest rival.

CHAPTER 4

MR. BIDEN GOES TO UKRAINE

CHINA, LUCRATIVE AS IT was, turns out to be only one source of Joe's and Hunter's incomes through corrupt means. Ukraine was the other.

Having begun their relationship with China in December 2014, Joe and Hunter traveled to Ukraine three months later. President Barack Obama had helpfully designated his vice president to be his point man in the effort to fight corruption there. The fox was appointed to guard the chicken coop.

DID JOE AND HUNTER GET $10 MILLION FROM UKRAINE?

The tale of Joe's and Hunter's corruption in Ukraine began in Washington, DC, on April 16, 2014, three months after their visit to Beijing, when the vice president met with Hunter's business partner, Devon Archer, at the White House.

Five days later, on April 21, 2014, Vice President Biden himself visited Ukraine. The next day, on April 22, 2014, Archer was appointed to the board of Burisma, the corrupt Ukraine energy company.

Things weren't going well for Burisma. On April 28, a week after Joe's visit to Ukraine, British officials raided the bank accounts of Burisma's owner, Mykola Zlochevsky. They seized $23 million.[1]

Often business executives under official investigation hire top lawyers to defend them, but Zlochevsky knew where true power resided and hired Hunter Biden on May 12 at a salary of $1 million per year, two weeks after his bank account was raided and emptied. It didn't matter that Hunter knew nothing about energy. Zlochevsky saw that Hunter was the key to Joe, and Joe was his get-out-of-jail-free card.

Meanwhile, the authorities closed in on Hunter's client and benefactor, Zlochevsky. At the end of 2014, he had to flee Ukraine amid allegations of unlawful bribery and money laundering. The next year, Zlochevsky's troubles mounted when Ukraine's prosecutor general Vitaly Yarema announced that he had been put on the wanted list for alleged financial corruption.[2]

But the Hunter connection seems to have worked. Magically, in February 2018, Zlochevsky was permitted to return to Ukraine after investigations into Burisma Holdings had been completed in December 2017. No charges were filed against him.

How did Zlochevsky do it? Were Hunter and Joe Biden his aces in the hole?

An informant revealed to the FBI that he thought so.[3]

On April 21, 2014, Air Force Two was flying to Kyiv, the capital of Ukraine. Aboard the flight were Jake Sullivan, the vice president's national security adviser, and Mike McCormick, a former White House stenographer for a decade. McCormick was also an FBI agent.

McCormick charges that the Bidens were deep into corruption in Ukraine. He told the *New York Post*, "Joe Biden committed crimes in Ukraine in a conspiracy with Jake Sullivan. I'm a witness to that happening."[4]

McCormick specifically shared that the timeline of events demonstrates that the vice president used his influence to help his son's foreign business interests: "Joe Biden was over there telling them, 'You can't be corrupt! You can't be corrupt!' while he was corrupt."

What did McCormick mean when he accused Biden and his national security adviser Jake Sullivan of corruption?

As of June 8, 2023, we can't be sure. But after months of dodging a document request by House Committee on Oversight and Reform chair James Comer (R-KY), the FBI confirmed the existence of an informant file, but so far, the bureau had given only limited access to members of the Oversight Committee. The file allegedly links President Joe Biden and Hunter to a $5 million bribery scheme. Comer said that the document concerns "policy decisions between now President Biden and a foreign national."[5]

We do not know yet if the document refers to McCormick's charges.

McCormick, as noted, spoke with Sullivan on the trip to Kyiv. McCormick says that Sullivan outlined how the US could help Ukraine rebuild its gas industry. McCormick says that Sullivan related to him how the US was interested in providing "technical assistance to help [Ukraine] be able to boost production in their conventional gas fields, where presently they aren't getting the maximum of what they could be" while offering "technical assistance relating to a regulatory framework, and also the technology that would be required to extract unconventional gas resources."[6]

If implemented, of course, these policies would greatly benefit Burisma.

In December 2014, amid broader Obama administration support for Ukraine, Congress approved $50 million to support the country's energy sector, including the natural gas industry—a boon for Burisma.[7]

MR. BIDEN GETS ZLOCHEVSKY'S PROSECUTOR FIRED

An FBI form (FD-1023)—filed to recount information from a confidential informant—sheds light on what went on in Ukraine between the Biden family and Zlochevsky. The information comes from a source who had been previously described by both Republicans and Democrats briefed on the matter as credible.

The source, as quoted in the FD-1023 form, details second-hand allegations that Burisma's CEO and founder, Mykola

Zlochevsky, thought having Hunter Biden on the board could help insulate the company from its problems with the prosecutor who was pursuing them.

It also alleges that Zlochevsky sent millions of dollars to Joe Biden as well as Hunter Biden and that two recordings about the matter exist that involve President Biden.

The information in the FD-1023 form was released by Sen. Chuck Grassley (R-IA) and House Oversight Republicans.[8]

The alleged bribes may have been connected with Ukrainian prosecutor Viktor Shokin, who was investigating Hunter Biden.

Joe Biden needed to get rid of Shokin. He was coming too close to discovering what was going on with Burisma and the Biden family's role in their corruption.

It is a matter of record that Vice President Biden, while carrying out Obama administration policy that had been coordinated with European allies, argued that Shokin was corrupt and threatened to withhold $1 billion in funding to Ukraine unless Shokin was fired.[9]

Hunter Biden at that time was on the board of Ukrainian energy company Burisma, which was the subject of an investigation by the prosecutor's office.

For Zlochevsky, the investigation came at an inconvenient time. He was trying to profit from an IPO (initial public offering) for Burisma and told the informant that if Shokin's investigation into Burisma were made public, it would have "a substantial negative impact on Burisma's prospective IPO."[10]

The informant said that Zlochevsky told him, "Don't worry, Hunter will take care of all those issues through his dad. . . . It cost $5 [million] to pay one Biden, and $5 [million] to another Biden."[11]

The FBI informant also said that during a meeting at Burisma's offices in late 2015 or 2016, Burisma chief financial officer Vadim Porjarskii said that Hunter Biden was hired to be on the board to "protect [them], through his dad, from all kinds of problems."[12]

Later, in a 2016 or 2017 phone call, Zlochevsky complained that he was "pushed to pay"[13] the Bidens, the FBI source said. Zlochevsky said he had recordings that showed that he was coerced into paying the Bidens to ensure that Shokin, the prosecutor, was fired—with a total of seventeen recordings, two of which involved Joe Biden.

Zlochevsky made clear that he did not send any funds directly to the "big guy," which investigators understood was a reference to Joe Biden. Zlochevsky additionally said it would take ten years to find all the bank records of illicit payments to Biden. Chairman James Comer (R-KY) says, "In the FBI's record, the Burisma executive [Zlochevsky] claims that he didn't pay the 'big guy' directly but that he used several bank accounts to conceal the money. That sounds an awful lot like how the Bidens conduct business: using multiple bank accounts to hide the source and total amount of the money."[14]

Democrats complain that the release of the FD-1023 form detailing the information provided by the informant risks human sources of intelligence. "We have repeatedly explained to Congress, in correspondence and in briefings, how critical it is to keep this source information confidential," the FBI said in a statement.[15]

They also question whether President Biden really called for prosecutor Shokin's ouster to help his son. They cite some reports that have said that the investigation of Burisma was, in fact, "dormant" by the time Biden called for Shokin's ouster.

But award-winning investigative journalist John Solomon confirmed, after an interview with Shokin, that he was fired because he got too close to exposing the Hunter-Joe-Burisma connection.

He told Solomon that at the time of Biden's intervention, his investigation was far from dormant. Solomon said that the prosecutor "told [him] he was making plans to question Hunter Biden about $3 million in fees that Biden and his partner, Archer, collected from Burisma through their American firm."[16]

Solomon wrote, "Former Vice President Joe Biden insists that he strong-armed Ukraine to fire its chief prosecutor solely because Biden believed that official was corrupt and inept, not because the Ukrainian was investigating a natural gas company, Burisma Holdings, that hired Biden's son, Hunter, into a lucrative job. . . . There's just one problem. Hundreds of pages of never-released memos and documents—many from inside the American team helping Burisma to stave off its legal troubles—conflict with Biden's narrative."[17]

Senators Chuck Grassley (R-IA) and Ron Johnson (R-WI) charge that "Burisma paid Hunter Biden and Archer over $4 million combined. A big chunk of it came during Joe Biden's vice presidency. And—mirabile dictu—it seems, for some unfathomable reason, that Hunter's salary was halved once his father was out of office."[18]

John Solomon wrote in the *Hill* in September 2019, "And they raise the troubling prospect that U.S. officials may have painted a false picture in Ukraine that helped ease Burisma's legal troubles and stop prosecutors' plans to interview Hunter Biden during the 2016 U.S. presidential election."[19]

Solomon writes, for instance, that Burisma's American legal representatives met with Ukrainian officials just days after Biden forced the firing of the country's chief prosecutor and had the gall to actually offer "an apology for dissemination of false information by U.S. representatives and public figures" about the Ukrainian prosecutors, according to the Ukrainian government's official memo of the meeting.[20]

The Obama administration knew full well of Hunter's activities in Ukraine and how close he skated to the edge of a conflict of interest—and then went over the line.

The Senate Finance Committee wrote that what it "discovered during the course of this investigation is that the Obama administration knew that Hunter Biden's position on Burisma's board was problematic and did interfere in the efficient execution of policy with respect to Ukraine. Moreover, this investigation has illustrated the extent to which officials within the Obama administration ignored the glaring warning signs when the vice president's son joined the board of a company owned by a corrupt Ukrainian oligarch."[21]

One further clue emerged that might help explain Zlochevsky's good fortune and a possible bribe to the Bidens.

In what the *New York Post* called "a remarkable coincidence" Ukrainian officials held a press conference on June 13,

2020—seventeen days before Comer's informant tipped him off—"where they showed off $5 million in cash allegedly offered as a bribe to end the investigation of Burisma's founder Mykola Zlochevsky."[22]

The *New York Post* reported that the "cash seized by Ukrainian officials in 2020 was paid in American $100 bills that were put on display—and matches the amount that Joe Biden allegedly received years earlier."[23]

So did Joe and Hunter Biden take $5 million each—or $10 million together—from Burisma owner Zlochevsky to persuade Ukraine to let him skate on corruption charges?

We don't have proof—yet—that Joe Biden did, but the evidence suggests a full criminal investigation of the matter is warranted.

Shokin says that the official explanation for his ouster—that he had not "adequately pursued corruption investigations" and that his efforts were essentially "dormant"—is bogus: "I can give very striking examples, namely our actions after the ban on $23 million Zlochevsky was lifted in the UK."[24]

Shokin continues, "I appointed an internal investigation, opened a criminal investigation into how—and why—the money that been seized was released in the UK. What is more, 10–12 days before my resignation, on February 2, 2016, the court seized assets, his personal savings, property, cars, and so on."[25]

Shokin said that the US intelligence agencies had been closely watching the investigation process, and he was confident that Biden was aware of the progress. Shokin added that he believed Biden acted behind the scenes to have him removed, fearing that the investigation could negatively affect his son and others close to him.

"I understand very well," Shokin added, "that the United States has one of the strongest intelligence agencies in the world. . . . Apparently, Mr. Biden was informed that we are approaching the moment when the interrogations of his son and other persons began."[26]

Shokin maintains that the real motivation behind Biden's push for his removal was to protect his personal and family interests rather than the interests of the American people.

We all remember the video of then vice president Joe Biden boasting of his role in Shokin's ouster, demanding his removal and threatening to withhold $1 billion in US aid to Ukraine unless Shokin was fired. "I looked at him [the Ukrainian government official who oversaw the Biden visit] and I said: I'm leaving in six hours. If the prosecutor is not fired, you're not getting the money. Well, son of a b*tch. He got fired," Biden said in 2018.[27]

As Shokin closed in on Burisma and Hunter, he found more and more evidence of corruption: "When we began to actively move forward with the aim of clarifying this crime and finding who had been guilty of violating Ukrainian laws at Burisma, we ended up discovering that the administrators recruited in May–June 2014 were probably involved. These were Devon Archer, Hunter Biden, and others. Joe Biden had reason to fear that all this would eventually fall on his son."[28]

BROTHER JAMES BIDEN GETS IN
ON THE ACTION

Meanwhile, brother James Biden, seven years Joe's junior, also got in on allegedly ripping off Ukraine. The Bidens boasted a close relationship with John Hynansky, a car dealer from Delaware. It was a reciprocal arrangement: the Bidens showered Hynansky with favors, and he gave them campaign contributions of tens of thousands of dollars.

Hynansky was particularly active in Ukraine, where he built a lucrative automobile import and dealership business.

Vice President Biden visited Kyiv in 2009 and took time, in his remarks, to single out Hynansky from his podium as his "very good friend." He noted that John was a "very prominent businessman in Delaware" and reported that he had had breakfast with him "the other day."

The laying on of hands sent the appropriate signals to the federal Overseas Private Investment Corporation (OPIC), whose board is appointed by the president with the mission of fostering job creation in the US through private investment.

OPIC showered Hynansky with loans. In July 2012, the corporation approved a $20 million loan to the car dealer to expand his import dealership, Winner Imports, in Ukraine.

Specifically, it was designed to "expand Winner Import Ukraine's automobile business and construct and operate two new state-of-the-art dealership facilities for Porsche and Land Rover/Jaguar automobiles."[29]

The investment had only one defect: OPIC's mandate was to create jobs in the United States, but the loan to Hynansky only created them in Ukraine.

But the investment paid other dividends to the Biden family.

It seems that James Biden had fallen on hard times. He owed $590,000 to the federal government in unpaid taxes. And in 2014, a contractor, Gator Pressure Cleaning and Custom Painting, slapped him with a $74,700 lien.

John Hynansky stepped up to the rescue and gave James two mortgages on his properties, totaling $900,000, from a Delaware company he controlled.

The transactional relationship came through for James. His debt to the IRS came down to only $30,000, and the Gator lien disappeared.

HUNTER AIDS A CORRUPT CLIENT IN AVOIDING US SANCTIONS FOR HELPING RUSSIA INVADE UKRAINE

Hunter famously had relations with Ukrainian billionaires in the past, including two who appear to have enjoyed special protection from the US government: Vladimir Yevtushenkov and Yelena Baturina. As the Biden administration imposed a slew of sanctions against Russians involved in helping Putin's war machine invade Ukraine, both mysteriously avoided suffering US sanctions.

Yevtushenkov's business empire Sistema recently included Russian rocket and radar maker RTI and drone maker Kronstadt, according to the *Daily Mail*. As the Russians invaded

Ukraine, observers expected Yevtushenkov to be sanctioned. "I think he should be sanctioned," Michael McFaul, a former US ambassador to Russia under President Barack Obama, told the *New York Post*.[30] Yevtushenkov's fortune is estimated by *Forbes* to be worth $1.7 billion.[31]

The reason for his escape from sanctions may be that despite Yevtushenkov being an odd dinner partner for a vice president of the United States, he *did* dine with then vice president Biden and Hunter—perhaps to discuss "favors" they might swap?[32]

EU Reporter noted that "despite his close links to the Kremlin, Vladimir Yevtushenkov seems untouched."[33]

Yevtushenkov, seventy-three, became the object of popular protests outside his London home when demonstrators waved placards and shouted, "Yevtushenkov is killing Ukraine."[34]

EU Reporter explained that his company, Kronshtadt—part of the Sistema Group—is said to be supplying Orion drones for Russian forces to bomb cities.[35] Critics say Yevtushenkov—with his inside Kremlin information about Russia looking to occupy Ukraine—invested heavily in the business.[36]

EU Reporter said that "being aware of the military plans of Ukraine, Yevtushenkov promptly invested in the production of military equipment. In 2015, a year after the 'Russian Spring,' Yevtushenkov acquired the Kronstadt Group, which specialized in the development of unmanned drones. For five years, Kronstadt Group has completely updated the Russia's defense line of drones. . . . And a year later, when a possible armed conflict between Ukraine and the country's Donbas region was widely anticipated, he quickly built a drone plant in Dubna."[37]

So with such involvement on the Russian side of the Russia–Ukraine War, why is Yevtushenkov sanctioned in the UK but not in the US?

After being hit with British sanctions, Yevtushenkov was forced to sell his controlling interest in his company, but he kept it in the family by selling it to his son.

Which brings us to another of Hunter and Joe's dinner partners.

Yevtushenkov's wife, Yelena Baturina, is a billionaire business-woman and the widow of the former corrupt mayor of Moscow. She enjoys a close relationship with the ubiquitous Hunter.

In 2012, during his father's vice presidency, Hunter Biden entered the real estate industry big time. He concocted a plan to acquire property in the US on behalf of Baturina. On February 14, 2014, Baturina wired Hunter's firm, Rosemont Seneca Thornton, $3.5 million for "consultancy services."

The money was paid to "enter the American [real estate] market," according to Yelena's brother, Viketo Baturin. The payment was flagged in a "suspicious activity report" by the US Department of the Treasury.[38]

Even more suspicious was Yelena's subsequent decision to wire $40 million to Hunter's firm through Inteco Management AG, a Swiss company she owned. This transaction was revealed in the "laptop from hell" left by the president's son at a computer repair shop in Atlanta.

Hunter had plans costing $69.7 million to invest in 2.5 million square feet of office space in Texas, Colorado, Alabama, New Mexico, and Oklahoma. This was partially financed by

Yelena's $40 million. Her company, Inteco Management AG, manufactures prefab housing materials and construction. At one point, Inteco Management AG was said to be responsible for 20 percent of the construction in Moscow.

According to cables published by WikiLeaks, the US ambassador to Russia, John Beyrle,[39] reported allegations that Baturina had links to major criminal groups, particularly Solntsevskaya Bratva.[40] Beyrle stated that her husband, former Moscow mayor Yury Luzhkov, sat on top of a "'pyramid' of corruption."[41]

Several Republican members of the Comer Oversight Committee questioned why Baturina was not sanctioned by the US. They wrote, "If the United States is avoiding sanctioning certain Russian oligarchs because of concerns they may attempt to influence American policy by exploiting Hunter Biden's connection with his father—the President of the United States—the American people deserve to know it. . . . If Hunter Biden's associates, including Elena Baturina, are being treated differently from other wealthy, politically connected Russians because of their connections with the President of the United States' son, the Administration should disclose this information to the American public."[42]

So to recap, Hunter's former partner, Devon Archer, testified that President Joe Biden met with Baturina, who then wired $3.5 million to Hunter for "consulting fees." Subsequently, Baturina invested $40 million in Hunter's real estate portfolio.

And the question still remains, Did President Biden's decision not to impose sanctions on Elena Baturina have anything to do with his son's relationship with her?

CHAPTER 5

MR. BIDEN GOES TO ROMANIA (AND HUNTER TRIES TO FREE A CORRUPT OLIGARCH)

IN 2014 AND 2015, while his father lectured officials in Kyiv about corruption, Hunter Biden was using his name to quash a corruption investigation in Romania against Gabriel Popoviciu, a real-estate tycoon ultimately convicted of paying a bribe to acquire a highly desirable lot at a bargain price. While Vice President Biden pressured Romania to ratchet up anticorruption prosecutions, Popoviciu paid Hunter Biden to use his connections to fend off the Romanian prosecutors.

Popoviciu paid Hunter $3 million, court records show, from his Cypriot company in return for Hunter's efforts to whitewash the corruption. Hunter used his family contacts and generous "referral fees" to opinion leaders to help his client get off.

As the House Committee documents, the payments were structured to conceal the fact that they were coming from

Popoviciu: multiple payments over time by the Romanian tycoon's business (Bladon Enterprises) to the Bidens' business partner, Rob Walker. Because smaller money transfers draw less regulatory attention, Walker parceled out Popoviciu's transfers into smaller payments and deposited them, over time, to various Hunter Biden accounts and accounts of business associates and even sent $10,000 to an account of Hallie Biden—Beau Biden's widow with whom Hunter was romantically involved. All in the family.[1]

Amazing how this works: after the vice president congratulated publicly President Klaus Iohannis on the strides Romania was making to crack down on corruption, Hunter privately stepped up his efforts to arrange a meeting between Romanian prosecutors and Popoviciu's lawyers—"perhaps in an effort to pay them off?"[2]

Popoviciu was convicted in a Romanian court in 2016 of bribing a university official to buy a 550-acre plot of government-owned land in a cut-price deal. He was sentenced to nine years. Even after this, Hunter didn't give up. He protested loudly for Popoviciu's innocence, writing in an email, "[Popoviciu] is, in my estimation, a very good man that's being very badly treated by a suspect Romanian justice system."[3] I'm sure you'll be shocked to hear that the Romanian courts didn't see it that way, upholding Popoviciu's nine-year prison sentence.[4]

Hunter then reached out to former FBI director Louis Freeh to help on the case by telling him, "[I am] working on a matter that I would like you to take a look at if you have the time." Hunter came to Freeh with plenty of money to back his cause:

"My client has never balked at bringing whatever team it takes together at whatever cost to obtain justice."[5]

The *Daily Mirror* notes that Hunter's team was "hired to organize a propaganda campaign to plant positive stories in the media on how their client was being treated unfairly by the Romanian justice system."[6]

Hunter and his associates cast a wide net for friends to help Popoviciu. One of Hunter's colleagues, Chris Boies, wrote to Hunter and his business partner Devon Archer to tell them that "one of my partners is best friends with the newly appointed Ambassador to Romania."[7]

Taking advantage of the opening, Hunter sought the help of then US ambassador to Romania Hans Klemm in what the *Daily Mail* called a "last-ditch effort to stop the corruption conviction."[8]

Central to their efforts to help Popoviciu was to have been a meeting with the Romanian anticorruption prosecutors. But the meeting never happened. As corrupt as Romania was, the government smelled a rat and would not meet with Hunter or his client.

Hunter's efforts were blown out of the water by an article in Politico praising Romanian prosecutors for cracking down on corruption. Hunter's associate Michael Gottlieb wrote, "This kind of article is likely to make our efforts with the USEMB [the US embassy] an uphill battle, and why I expect HK [Klemm] has had little interest in taking any kind of public position."[9]

But with Hunter's encouragement, Freeh persisted in trying to use his contacts to get Popoviciu off. Popoviciu's retainer agreement with Freeh was evidence that the Romanian would do whatever it took, at whatever cost, to get off the hook.

Freeh was not above hinting at a payoff to free his new client, noting that Popoviciu "owns a half a billion real estate development." Freeh suggested that they hire someone to do a report defending Popoviciu and then use "that report to establish a dialogue with the prosecutor—resulting in some possible deal or remediated outcome." In other words, a bribe.

Undaunted, the former FBI director quickly brought his extensive law enforcement contacts to bear to help the tycoon.

The *Daily Mail* describes Freeh's frantic work to get his client off: "Flaunting his international connections, he wrote to Hunter on June 21: 'I will see my good friend, Ron Noble [the former secretary general of international police organization Interpol], in NY on Thursday and most likely he knows this DNA [Romanian anticorruption office] chief prosecutor, Laura Codruta Kobesi, very well. . . . Let me talk to him and see what the possibilities may be to meet with her and to initiate a dialogue which would remediate the situation. I want to make sure I can add some value to this equation before proceeding.'"[10]

Next, Freeh emailed Hunter to report that he had spoken with the head of the FBI's criminal division about the case—and offered to pay Hunter a referral fee for involving him.

"I wanted to thank you again for referring Gabriel to us and we have finalized an attorney letter of engagement with him," Freeh wrote to the then vice president's son two weeks after Popoviciu was sentenced to nine years in prison.[11] "I will meet him in Paris Sunday and then we'll deploy to Bucharest and get to work."[12]

Freeh added helpfully, "FYI, I have had conversations with the head of the FBI's Criminal Division and there is a sincere Bureau interest in meeting and debriefing Gabriel on other matters he may be willing to discuss. FBIHQ will relay its interest to the Legat [legal attaché] in Bucharest, with whom we'll meet next week. . . . We have fortunately been able to enlist for our team a former FBI Legat in Bucharest—she's Romanian-American—who is a fluent speaker with excellent SRI contacts. We may also try to see the Ambassador."

In the email, Freeh also offered to give a referral payment to Hunter for getting him the job with Popoviciu: "I would also like to make a small payment to you for this referral—and for your continuing work on this matter. . . . This is a standard practice. It's strictly your call as I don't know your relationship with the client. We would just need your bank information in order to make a remittance."[13] The saga ended when police showed up at Popoviciu's Romanian home to find that the real estate mogul had fled. He was later arrested in London in August 2017.

While his son was doing his allegedly corrupt business in Romania, Vice President Joe Biden visited Romania to condemn just the sort of dishonesty his son was practicing. Excoriating public malfeasance, Joe piously proclaimed that "corruption is just another form of tyranny."[14]

About the Romanian payments to Hunter, the *Washington Free Beacon* reported, "Many Republicans have expressed frustration that prosecutors have ignored Biden's foreign business dealings, or what appears to be his unregistered foreign lobbying. The Lobbying Disclosure Act requires individuals to disclose their lobbying activity to Congress, and the Foreign Agents Registration Act requires them to disclose lobbying on behalf of foreign nationals like Popoviciu to the Justice Department."[15]

Romania has one of the saddest experiences with corruption anywhere in the world. Under their communist dictator Nicolae Ceaușescu, the Romanian people suffered unbelievable repression.[16]

With the economy in free fall, desperate for revenue, Ceaușescu took to treating his people as livestock to be used for his personal profit. Prohibiting both abortion and birth control, Ceaușescu set up a lucrative business selling human body parts and organs "harvested" from newborn babies in the regime's inhumane network of juvenile internment institutions.

Between 1966 and Ceaușescu's fall in 1989, an estimated fifteen thousand to twenty thousand children died unnecessarily.

The *Guardian* reports, "The country's orphanages began to fill up from the late 1960s, when the state decided to battle a demographic crisis by banning abortion and removing contraception from sale. Many of those in the orphanages were not actually orphans, but those whose parents felt they could not cope financially with raising a child. . . . The most horrific abuse took place in homes for disabled children, who were taken away from their families and institutionalized."[17]

A report by the European Parliament in 2015 named Romania as a source and transit country for organ trafficking. Kidneys sold for $6,000 each, and other organs were trafficked as well.[18]

In this filthy cesspool of human degradation and corruption, Hunter Biden fit right in, using his father's credentials as the official corruption fighter in Eastern Europe to make money dishonestly.

CHAPTER 6

MR. BIDEN GOES TO KAZAKHSTAN

ONE OF HUNTER'S FRIENDS is Kenes Rakishev, whose close ties to the kleptocratic regime of Kazakhstan's despotic former president Nursultan Nazarbayev made him an especially attractive mark for the vice president's son.

Joe Biden can't deny being involved in this particular Hunter escapade because of an undated photo, first published in 2019, of Joe with Hunter and Rakishev.[1]

Between 2012 and 2014, the *Daily Mail* reports, "[The emails] passed to this newspaper via anti-corruption campaigners from the Central Asian country reveal that Biden Jr. held extensive meetings with Rakishev, who was looking to invest a portion of his personal fortune in New York and Washington DC. He also travelled to the Kazakh capital of Astana to hold business discussions. . . . Hunter Biden then attempted to persuade Rakishev to buy into a Nevadan mining company, brokering a series of meetings with the firm."[2]

That deal fell through, but then Hunter, ever resourceful when it came to corrupt deals with Biden officials, convinced the oligarch to invest $1 million with Alexandra Forbes Kerry, the filmmaker daughter of Democrat 2004 presidential candidate and future secretary of state John Kerry.

Rakishev, who wrote messages in broken English, appears to have become intimate with the vice president's son, calling Hunter "my brother!" and "my brother from another mother!"

They shared gossip about their family holidays and dined together at luxury restaurants in New York and Washington, DC ("I'm on vacation with family [at] Lake Michigan . . . trying to spend some much-needed time with my wife and daughters. It's my 20th anniversary of marriage tomorrow," Hunter told Rakishev in July 2013).[3]

Rakishev eventually succeeded in acquiring vast wealth, appearing on *Forbes*'s top-fifteen list of Kazakhstan's "most influential tycoons," his assets estimated at $332 million.

The *Daily Mail* reports, "Like many an oligarch in possession of a huge fortune, Rakishev was now looking for a safe place to park it, so had come to America in search of new places to invest his hard-earned roubles."[4]

But the *Daily Mail* laments, "Sadly, things hadn't gone entirely smoothly. For in the highly regulated world of Western capitalism, Rakishev discovered that blue-chip investment partners were often reluctant to take his cash. To blame? The fact that no one was entirely sure where his wealth actually came from."[5]

The International Finance Corporation, a highly respectable sister organization of the World Bank, "politely informed the oligarch that it 'cannot invest with him' because its 'very deep due diligence processes' had established that he had some 'connections' involving the 'president's family' that 'are a liability to us.'"[6]

Rakishev, outraged, ranted that he would see to it that the organization "never works in Kazakhstan with anyone."[7]

The US Department of Justice then took notice of Rakishev and launched an investigation of potential breaches of the Foreign Corrupt Practices Act related to "an investment in the oil and gas industry in Kazakhstan."[8]

The investigation led Rakishev to reach out to Hunter Biden for help. Responding to his pleas, in May 2012, Devon Archer emailed the disgraced oligarch: "Can you have dinner with me, Hunter Biden, Alex [Forbes Kerry] and team on Wednesday next week in NYC? I want to let Hunter know when he should come up from DC to see you on Wednesday. Looking forward to seeing you!"[9]

Rakishev replied, "Hi Devon! I would be happy to have a dinner with you and all our friends! Thank you very much for invitations! Take care my brother!"[10]

The *Daily Mail* continued to chronicle the Biden-Rakishev saga: "By July, Hunter had travelled to Astana to discuss business opportunities. 'I wanted to check in with you and see what our next steps are to follow up on our visit to Kazakhstan,' he wrote in an email to Rakishev sent shortly afterwards. 'Let me know if you need anything from me.' Three months later, Biden was helping Rakishev hold discussions about investing in Prospect Global Resources, a potash mining firm based in eastern Arizona."[11]

Then in late October 2013, Archer arranged a conference call between Rakishev and Alex Forbes Kerry, who was by then attempting to raise cash to launch her film production firm, Fictional Pictures.

Immediately after the call that December, Rakishev emailed with happy news: "Thank you my brother from another mother! Thanks, you very much my brother! We decided to invest 1 mln [million]! Give them my email!"[12]

The *Daily Mail* reports, "Ms. Forbes Kerry, who has never publicly acknowledged her debt to Rakishev, finalized the deal in January 2014. The following month, she and Biden met Rakishev for dinner in Washington DC."[13]

"It was a pleasure to meet you with Devon and Hunter the other day," she told him by email afterward. "I want to thank you for the beautiful watch! I am sorry I didn't open it at the table. I misunderstood and thought it was a baby present, so I only opened it when I was at home. It is absolutely beautiful, and you are so generous. . . . Please come to New York soon and bring your family. We will host you and your team."

"Rakishev responded that he intended to take up that offer in September. 'Let's be in touch!' he wrote."[14]

And so the Biden family's tour of the world continued. Next stop: Costa Rica, with a brief detour to California.

CHAPTER 7

MR. BIDEN GOES TO CALIFORNIA, GETS SOMEONE KILLED, AND GETS AWAY WITH IT

THE BIDEN FAMILY HAS many tentacles apart from Hunter. Joe's younger brother Frank figures prominently.

Frank got off to a bad start.

In 1999, Frank's driver's license was suspended, but despite this impediment, he rented a Jaguar XK8 sports car. On August 14, 1999, Frank drove with a young friend, Jason Thurton, to a midnight concert at the Belly Up Tavern in Cardiff, California. Without a license, Frank gave the car keys to Jason. Peter Schweizer recounts, "Frank rode shotgun, handled the stick shift, and provided instructions as they cruised down the highway. At one point, Frank shifted into high gear and told Jason 'to punch the car and leave it in third gear' until told otherwise. Frank then gave the command for fourth gear and the Jaguar picked up speed. Soon they were humming along at 70–80 mph in a 35 mph zone."[1]

Then the joyride turned gruesome. Schweizer resumes his narrative: "Michael Albano, a 37-year-old single father, was crossing the street . . . when the car rammed into him. Albano was first struck by the right headlamp which sent him crashing into the windshield, over the top of the car, into a backseat passenger's face, and then into the Jaguar's trunk before landing on the asphalt." Two witnesses say Frank urged Jason to "keep driving."[2]

Albano died at the scene, leaving behind two daughters. Jason pled guilty to a hit-and-run, and the guardians of Albano's daughters sued Frank in a civil wrongful death lawsuit. Frank skipped. "He never showed up at the courthouse, did not answer any of the legal correspondence, and never replied to the court's final order in September 2002, awarding the Albano family $275,000 for each of the two daughters."[3]

"The Albanos had to hire a private detective to find Frank. The Biden family attorney refused to provide any information on Frank's whereabouts or to even accept service of the documents." Frank was, according to witnesses, holed up at brother Joe's house while Joe was serving in the Senate.[4]

The Albano girls never did collect the judgment. The guardians contacted the senator eight years after the accident, who handed their request off to an aide, who wrote back, "The Senator wishes to express his deep sympathy with the Albano daughters over their loss."[5]

Then came the brushoff: "While it is correct, as you state, that Senator Biden was not involved in the accident and bears no legal liability for the judgment, the Senator would certainly encourage his brother to pay the judgment if his personal financial circumstances made that at all possible. As you are aware, however, Frank has no assets with which to satisfy the judgment. The Senator regrets that this is where matters stand and that he cannot be more helpful."[6]

In fact, Joe's protestation that Frank was broke and could not pay the judgment was false, and Joe knew it. Seven days before the Albano daughters' guardians contacted Senator Biden to solicit his help in getting his brother to pay what he owed, Frank Biden was hit with a federal tax lien for $23,000. You don't get a tax lien for unpaid income taxes if you don't earn any income!

So where was Frank Biden? He was busy making money in Costa Rica, one of the few countries that did not have an agreement with the US, so US courts couldn't touch Frank or enforce the verdict for the daughters of the man he helped kill.

CHAPTER 8

MR. BIDEN GOES TO COSTA RICA

COSTA RICA BECKONED FRANK. In late March 2009, Costa Rican president—and future Nobel Prize winner—Oscar Arias met with Vice President Joe Biden to beg for more aid from the US.

Costa Rica loomed large in Frank Biden's future ever since President Obama appointed Vice President Joe Biden to focus on helping the region, just as he had in Ukraine and Romania.

How convenient for Frank Biden, who was already working at the time with the Costa Rican National Energy and Light Company (CNFL) on a massive project called Guanacaste Solar Park. CNFL had picked Frank's company, Sun Fund Americas, to work with them on the project, even though he had no background in energy. But he had a prominent last name, and that was all the credentials he needed.

Frank had big dreams for Costa Rica. He envisioned build-ing "thousands of homes in the jungles of Costa Rica, a world-class golf course, casinos, and an anti-aging center."[1] Frank's last name provided entry to the country's ministries of education, energy, and the environment and produced a meeting with the new president of Costa Rica, Luis Guillermo Solís Rivera.

Whatever social movement was sweeping Washington, from providing aid to Central America to implementing solar energy to improving home construction in the Costa Rican jungles, Frank Biden was there, flaunting his name and cutting himself in. As President Obama's focus homed in on solar energy pro-duction in the Caribbean, Frank was right there pushing Sun Fund Americas.

It was similar to that famous Marx Brothers movie, *At the Circus*, wherein Groucho, playing an attorney named J. Cheever Loophole, rubs his hands in glee after hearing about a lucra-tive deal and exclaims, "There must be some way I can get a piece of that."[2]

Frank's projects moved forward rapidly, with the Biden name acting as a very effective lubricant. In 2015, the Obama admin-istration's OPIC authorized a $6.5 million, taxpayer-backed loan to advance Frank's Costa Rican project.

The next year, the Costa Rican Ministry of Public Education signed a letter of intent with Sun Fund Americas to operate solar power facilities in the country.

Frank's success in Costa Rica whetted his ambitions for more investments in Central America. When Vice President Biden announced the launch of the Caribbean Energy Security

Initiative (CESI) in June 2014, Frank was the first in line. Backed by US loan guarantees, Frank Biden's Sun Fund Americas announced plans to build a twenty-megawatt solar facility in Jamaica. The US ambassador said that the project would not have been possible without OPIC financing.[3]

Even though Frank Biden had obviously recovered from his poverty, he had no money to spare for the Albano daughters, who still have not gotten a dime from him.

CHAPTER 9

MR. BIDEN GOES TO FLORIDA

WHEN OBAMA BECAME PRESIDENT, he pledged to double the funding for charter schools. While traditionally, Democrats have treated charter schools with suspicion, worried that they would divert federal funds from public schools and reduce the ranks of union-dues-paying teachers, Obama defied the trend and pushed for charters.

As always, Frank Biden wanted in on the kill.

In 2009, the year his brother became vice president, Frank scored when he ran into a local Florida business executive at a Starbucks. Over coffee, the executive asked if Joe's little brother would become the new president and frontman for a fledging charter school venture.

While Frank had no experience in the field—any more than Hunter knew his way around an oil field when he joined the energy company Burisma's board in Ukraine—he jumped at the chance to make a buck.

ABC News describes how Frank "touted his famous last name and prominent connections in Washington to help land the company a series of charter contracts from local officials in Florida to open charter schools, earning hundreds of thousands of dollars over a five-year period from the company in the process."[1]

Frank wasn't shy about floating his name around. In an interview, he said his last name was "a tremendous asset" that brought him "automatic acceptance as he sought government approvals for his for-profit charter school company called Mavericks in Education."[2]

Frank's job was to secure contracts with local Florida school boards to bring in Mavericks in Education to run charter schools in their districts. ABC News explains, "Charter schools are heavily regulated and depend on approvals by school boards and other government officials to operate, so convincing school board members of the company's viability was a critical step for nascent charter management outfits. That was Frank Biden's job for Mavericks."[3]

Spreading his famous name around among school board members and government officials did the trick, and Mavericks in Education won contracts throughout the state. Frank was reportedly paid $70,000 a year by the chain.

One Mavericks in Education board member recounts how "Frank Biden wore cufflinks bearing the presidential seal to meetings, and during a commencement address for one of the schools' graduation ceremonies, he 'spoke about his brother and about how his brother was the vice president. It was all about his brother.'"[4]

But all did not end well for Mavericks in Education: "Since opening their doors, schools operated by Mavericks in Education have been mired in controversy, struggled with performance, and, in lawsuits and state audits, faced allegations of fraudulent activity."[5]

A lawsuit in 2014 brought by Pinellas County school district officials accused Mavericks in Education of "falsely inflating the operating expenses associated with the operations of the charter schools" to "divert funds from the education of the students to the owners of [Mavericks in Education]" to the tune of $22 million.[6]

In 2012, a former teacher at the Mavericks school in Palm Beach filed a whistleblower lawsuit accusing her supervisors at the company of altering student enrollment records to secure more government funding.

ABC News explains, "Charter school management companies like Mavericks operate a network of publicly funded but independently operated schools. Funding for schools is measured on the number of students enrolled at each school."[7]

Padding the enrollment data to get more state money is an old trick, and Florida school officials caught on to what was happening at Mavericks in Education. In 2017, they forced the company to sell its contracts to manage charter schools to EdisonLearning, another charter school management company. When Mavericks in Education was dismissed, it operated six schools with twenty-five hundred students. EdisonLearning disbanded the schools' boards of directors and dismissed management.

But Mavericks in Education not only failed because it inflated its enrollment; it also struck out in the classroom too. Graduation rates at Mavericks in Education schools were far below the state average. Its most successful school graduated just one-third of its students, while the worst graduated just 14 percent.

In periodic reviews posted online by the Florida Department of Education—which indicate whether a charter school is improving, maintaining, or declining in educational standards—the Mavericks in Education schools were among those that received ratings of "unsatisfactory" or "declining."

Mavericks in Education schools got terrible ratings from state regulators. Schweizer reports, "From 2009 to 2014, individual schools received 'declining' ratings three times and, one year got an F."[8]

Frank Biden's record of failure at Mavericks in Education reflected his real priorities: using his famous name to get paid as a frontman for marketing. Whether the company offered a quality education was not his concern.

In fact, the Mavericks in Education schools offered an abysmal education. Schweizer recounts how "students would interact with teachers for only a few hours each day. The rest of the time, they would sit in front of computers in what was euphemistically called 'self-directed' learning."[9]

Frank candidly explained that he was not going to make much money from the schools themselves; the real money was in the real estate on which they sat. "It's all about the buildings we buy," Frank explained. "Certainly, the operation of the schools isn't profitable."[10]

So Frank spun off from getting state accreditation for schools to managing their properties. He became a partner in School Property Development, which provided services to Mavericks in Education schools, and owned the property on which they were situated.

Frank boasted that the companies he owned or controlled "are responsible for over $12 billion in school financing placed with over 200 schools built and operated in Florida."[11]

Frank had found a gold mine. His strategy was to charge the charter schools a high enough rent to pay off the mortgage on the property. Schweizer writes, "In short, the schools were a vehicle for Frank's firm School Property Development LLC to profit from buying or leasing real estate from [Mavericks in Education]." He explains, "Because the schools were using taxpayer money and receiving grants to pay for the buildings, they were probably less concerned with the cost of rent."[12]

But the entire scam rested on massive infusions of government money, brought to the schools by the brother of the vice president of the United States. As of 2015, each Mavericks in Education school was getting a quarter of a million dollars in government subsidy.

With hypocrisy beyond compare, Vice President Joe Biden told crowds on the campaign trail in Texas, "I do not support any federal money for for-profit charter schools period. The bottom line is that it siphons off money from public schools which are already in enough trouble."[13]

He neglected to mention that his brother was one of the main people doing the siphoning.

Frank Biden's parasitic relationship with education—as with solar energy and a host of other projects—bespeaks a sociopath who apparently regards any social cause, no matter how idealistic, as a potential moneymaker and little else.

While Joe Biden provided rhetorical cover by extolling the virtues of charter schools and solar power, Frank Biden sat in the back room raking in the money.

Unfortunately, even this vast accumulation of wealth was not adequate for Frank to see his way clear to helping the two young girls whom he left as orphans while he was joyriding in his Jaguar. The fact that Frank's conscience did not bother him leads us to the inexorable conclusion that he hasn't got one.

Chapter 10

MR. BIDEN GOES TO IRAQ

A WAR-TORN COUNTRY, DESPERATELY in need of vast reconstruction? The ideal target for the Biden family.

But this time, it was James Biden, seven years Joe's junior, who led the plunder.

Hillstone International, a multinational construction company founded in 1976, was hemorrhaging money in 2011, just as the reconstruction of Iraq moved into high gear.[1]

The company president, Kevin Justice, was a longtime Biden friend who grew up in Delaware. On November 4, 2010, Justice visited the White House. Was it just coincidence that less than three weeks later, Hillstone announced that it would have a new executive vice president, James Biden? Lacking any experience in construction, Hillstone publicized James's arrival at the firm by noting his "forty years of experience dealing with principals in business, political, legal and financial circles."

It was that experience that helped Hillstone land a six-year contract with the US Army of Engineers. Iraq was only one of the places where James won contracts. He also succeeded in getting business in Puerto Rico, Mozambique, and elsewhere.

CHAPTER 11

MR. BIDEN GOES OFF THE RESERVATION

THE OGLALA SIOUX ARE one of the poorest tribes in the US. And thanks to being ripped off by Hunter and his best buddy Devon Archer, they are now poorer still. Burnham Financial Group was accused by the feds of "orchestrating a scheme to defraud investors and a Native American tribal entity of tens of millions of dollars."[1]

The fraud targeted pension funds that had "socially responsible investing" clauses, including union pension funds that had been given to Joe Biden's campaigns in the past. Eleven pension funds were defrauded in the scheme, including eight that represented government employees.

The honor roll of defrauded pension funds includes the following:

- Birmingham, Alabama, Water Works Pension Plan
- Chicago Transit Authority
- Management International Longshoremen's Association
- Milk Drivers and Dairy Employees Local Union No. 246
- Omaha, Nebraska, School Employees Retirement Fund
- Philadelphia Housing Authority
- Richmond, Virginia, Retirement System
- Washington Suburban Sanitary Commission

CHAPTER 12

MS. BIDEN GOES
TO WASHINGTON

IT WASN'T JUST THE Biden boys who swam in the corrupt waters of Washington and other countries.

Joe's sister, Valerie, cashed in too.

One of the anomalies of the federal campaign finance system that drives candidates crazy is that the candidate must separate his own money from the campaign's funds. Many a candidate consigns himself to poverty while his campaign luxuriates in massive funding. However, it is illegal to dip into the campaign funds to pay for personal expenses.

To the Biden family, the solution lay in Valerie Biden, Joe's sister.

Valerie signed on as an "executive vice president" consultant to Joe Slade White & Company, the firm responsible for buying the advertising for Joe Biden's campaign. Under the arrangement, which is customary in political campaigns, the consulting firm working for the candidate draws a commission of up to 15 percent of the total media spending.[1]

The total payments to Joe Slade White & Company came to two and a half million dollars from "Citizens for Biden" and "Biden for President" campaigns between March 2007 and October 2008.[2] We don't know how much Valerie made in just that twenty-month period, but one can image it was sizable.

Joe Slade White & Company and Valerie were a team that have worked together throughout Joe's career, a span of eighteen years.

Valerie signed on as an "executive vice president" consultant to Joe Slade White & Company, the firm responsible for buying the advertising for Joe Biden's campaign. Under the arrangement, which was customary in political campaigns, the consulting firm working for the candidate draws a commission of up to 15 percent of the total media spending.

When it came to using his family to game the system and make money, Joe and company never missed a trick.

CHAPTER 13

MR. BIDEN GOES TO THE IRS

FEDERAL PROSECUTORS WERE CONSIDERING charging Hunter with three tax crimes and a charge related to a gun purchase. NBC News reported, "The possible charges are two misdemeanor counts for failure to file taxes, a single felony count of tax evasion related to a business expense for one year of taxes, and the gun charge, also a potential felony."[1]

But federal prosecutors have expressed frustration at the slow pace of the probe: "Two senior law enforcement sources told NBC News about 'growing frustration' inside the FBI because investigators finished the bulk of their work on the case about a year ago. A senior law enforcement source said the IRS finished its investigation more than a year ago."[2]

The *Washington Post* reported that federal investigators believed they had gathered enough evidence to charge Hunter

Biden with tax crimes and a false statement related to a gun purchase.[3]

NBC News said, "The federal investigation of Hunter Biden began in 2018. It has narrowed from an inquiry into his international business relationships, including any possible national security implications, to an examination of the income he earned from those ventures and a false statement he's alleged to have made during the gun purchase."[4]

In 2018, during a period when he admitted to using cocaine, Hunter Biden purchased a firearm, which required him to fill out a form that included a question about whether he was addicted to or abusing any unlawful substance.[5] Not surprisingly, Hunter lied.

But according to *USA Today*, the pressure on Hunter escalated when a whistleblower at the IRS, a criminal supervisory special agent who was investigating Hunter, told lawmakers that the special agent and his "entire team [were] removed from the probe," which caused all eyes to turn to Hunter's activities.[6]

In a letter from his lawyers, Joseph Ziegler, an IRS criminal investigator, said he "was informed that he and his entire investigative team are being removed from the ongoing and sensitive investigation of the high-profile, controversial subject about which [Ziegler] sought to make whistleblower disclosures to Congress."[7]

After the whistleblower's revelation, IRS Commissioner Daniel Werfel confirmed that the team of investigators had been fired and added that it was at the direction of the Department of Justice.

Lawyers for the undisclosed whistleblower charged that "this move is clearly retaliatory and may also constitute obstruction of a congressional inquiry. . . . Our client has a right to make disclosures to Congress. Any attempt by any government official to prevent a federal employee from furnishing information to Congress is also a direct violation of longstanding appropriations restriction."[8]

Meanwhile, a second whistleblower, Gary Shapley, a fourteen-year veteran of the IRS, also attacked the service in public, saying that the investigation of Hunter Biden was deliberately delayed. "There were multiple steps that were slow-walked—were just completely not done—at the direction of the Department of Justice," he charged. "When I took control of this particular investigation, I immediately saw deviations from the normal process. It was way outside the norm of what I've experienced in the past."[9]

Shapley is a supervisory special agent with the IRS's Criminal Investigations Department, currently operated by a team of twelve agents who specialize in international tax and financial crimes. Previously, he was an officer with the National Security Agency's Office of the Inspector General. He was assigned to a "sensitive" investigation in January 2020 (the Hunter Biden probe), and within months, he said he grew concerned about how the Justice Department was handling the investigation.

As of this writing, Hunter has pled guilty to the equivalent of a speeding ticket. He admitted failing to file two years of tax returns and lying on his gun application.

He will not see the inside of a jail and will get off with the lightest of slaps on the wrist.

Or not? A funny thing happened when Justice Department prosecutors and Hunter's defense counsel appeared in the courtroom of US district judge Maryellen Noreika to get official approval of the sweetheart plea deal they had reached to let Hunter off the hook: Judge Noreika asked the Justice Department if Hunter would face any additional charges if she bought into the plea deal. Hearing that this was it and that Hunter would be off the hook, she balked, saying that "she couldn't find another example of a diversion agreement so broad that it shielded the defendant from charges in a different case."

The deal was dead, and it remains to be seen if the so-called Justice Department will pursue Hunter on his many alleged crimes.

CHAPTER 14

WILL MR. BIDEN GO TO JAIL?

WHICH ONE? JOE OR Hunter? For either, though, don't bet on it. The possible charges against Hunter Biden all rest squarely under the jurisdiction of federal employees directly appointed by President Biden. Whether in the US Attorney's Office, the Department of Justice, or the IRS, it is Biden appointees who have the power of "prosecutorial discretion" to decide whether and about what to charge Hunter.

President Biden and the Justice Department have resisted fiercely requests that he appoint a special prosecutor to investigate his son and other members of his family. Until or unless the president is forced to appoint a special prosecutor, it is very unlikely that serious criminal charges will ever be brought against Hunter Biden.

But in August 2023, Attorney General Merrick Garland bowed to intense pressure and finally named a special counsel (prosecutor) to investigate the Bidens. But the man he appointed, David Weiss, is the guy who oversaw the investigation of Hunter by the DOJ that led to the sweetheart plea deal just rejected by Judge Noreika.

Joe Biden, if the charge that he got a $5 million bribe pans out, will be subject to impeachment. And if the charges are true, you can bet he will be impeached in the House with even some Democratic votes. But no way will he be convicted in the Senate and be removed from office. The more likely course is that he is forced to step aside from the 2024 election by angry Republicans and terrified Democrats.

Prison? Nope. Impeachment is the only remedy you can use against a president or a vice president.

But the larger question is why Hunter, James, and Frank Biden were allowed to get away with such open and blatant conflicts of interest.

US law, enacted after decades of conflict-of-interest scandals, is quite explicit in the disclosure requirements on elected and appointed officials. The penalties for violation are severe.

For decades, corrupt politicians have hidden behind their spouses to shield their larceny from public view. But in 1994, the ethics code (18 U.S.C. § 208) was passed to include spouses in the requirements: "Your spouse's financial interests are considered your financial interests under this statute the government explained."[1]

But sons, daughters, mothers, fathers, brothers, and sisters have never been covered.

So Hunter, James, and Frank Biden may skate on a big loophole in the law.

We need to plug that loophole and apply federal ethics standards and disclosure to other family members.

But this loophole in the law doesn't mean the Biden family will get off without exposure.

To recap where we are now, the revelations of the corruption of the Biden family are, as you read this, reverberating around the country. It seems very likely that the House of Representatives will impeach President Biden.

Undoubtedly, the hearings attendant to this impeachment will shed new light on the family's corruption and tie it directly to the president. With the House firmly in Republican control, it is almost certain that the House will vote to impeach Biden.

But with the Senate in Democratic hands, it is equally certain to acquit him, leaving him in office.

Then the voters will get their chance to weigh in.

As Biden faces serious charges of corruption, the country is watching a circus, by comparison, in the other rink, where the Department of Justice, New York District Attorney Alan Bragg, and Fulton County DA Fani Willis have indicted former president Trump on—pardon me—*trumped*-up charges. These indictments are not likely to be tried or adjudicated until after the 2024 elections. But if by chance the biased all-Democrat juries that will hear the cases in Manhattan, DC, and Fulton County do return verdicts of conviction, they will likely be reversed on appeal.

So the election will probably pit a candidate who has been indicted against one who has been impeached.

The charges against Trump fall into two categories.

Some are highly technical charges that he may or may not have committed picayune violations of law. One charge says that he listed payments to porn actress Stormy Daniels as a business expenditure instead of a campaign expenditure—the wrong line on the form. Another alleges that he failed to return documents to the National Archives. But absent any indication that he compromised national security by keeping them, it is hard to discern what grand criminal violation is being prosecuted. He is being charged, in effect, with no more than having an overdue library book! And in my estimation, based on known facts, President Biden, although unprosecuted, is guilty of the same thing.

The other charges are more significant and dangerous to our democracy. Prosecutors are charging that by expressing his opinion that he won the 2020 election and that the official result was "rigged," he was more than just exercising his right to free speech; he was actively trying to overturn an election and overthrow the government. His efforts to prove that illegal shenanigans led to his defeat in 2020 are falsely being portrayed as a conspiracy to reverse an election result, his lawyers maintain. If the DOJ can criminalize a president for his speech, we no longer live in a democracy.

But the charges against Biden are far more serious than those against Trump. More than violations of law, they may have also compromised the presidency and our government to give real aid and comfort to our leading foreign enemy—China.

PART 3

HOW CHINA GOT ITS MONEY'S WORTH FROM THE BIDENS

CHAPTER 15

BIDEN LETS CHINA OFF
THE HOOK FOR COVID-19

WHEN TRUMP ENTERED THE final year of his presidency, the United States was in the middle of an upswing, second only, perhaps, to the "It's Morning Again in America" economic boom of the Reagan presidency.

Trump had created seven million new jobs. Unemployment had dropped from 4.7 percent to 3.5 percent at the end of Trump's third year. The economy had grown by 3 percent a year. Trump seemed poised to win an easy reelection victory based on one of the more successful records of modern times.

But China could not permit Trump to win again. Trump's pro-growth policies and his successful efforts to cut China's trade surplus had slowed Beijing's economy after years of record growth.

China's gross domestic product (GDP) growth rate had slowed from 14 percent in 2008 to 10 percent in 2010 to

6 percent in 2019, and many doubting the government's figures put it at an even slower pace. Exports had dropped 12 percent since Trump imposed tariffs, and Beijing feared an even steeper drop coming. China's unemployment rate grew from 4.2 percent to 5 percent as Trump entered his final year.

But the prospects for beating Trump were dim.

Perhaps the answer to China's problems lay in a lab in Wuhan, China, where the military had been conducting gain-of-function research, or studying how to increase a normal virus's lethality and ability to infect humans.[1]

In January 2020, a few lab workers in Wuhan got sick with the COVID-19 virus. Later that month, it spread to the US. By the time it had completed its ravages, over a million Americans had died, and with businesses locked down, the American economy had crumbled.

China, too, was hit hard, losing 121,000 people, but nothing like the losses in the US.

The World Health Organization (WHO) probed the source of the virus, but beyond knowing that it had originated in the Wuhan lab, they could not identify how it had spread to humans.

The Chinese government maintained that it spread through the bite of a bat from the nearby wet market in the city, but a hearing by the Select Subcommittee on the Coronavirus Pandemic found that the theory that the virus stemmed from a leak in the Wuhan lab rather than from a stray bat was "the only credible explanation or the origin of COVID-19."[2]

Unfortunately, scientific witnesses who testified before the subcommittee "also detailed the politicization of the lab leak hypothesis by intelligence community officials who were afraid to align with the beliefs of the Republican administration."[3]

For its part, China kept data that might have confirmed or refuted the lab leak theory hidden. The head of the WHO noted, "This data could have and should have been shared three years ago. We continue to call on China to be transparent in sharing data and to conduct the necessary investigations and share results."[4]

A special investigative committee, set up by the WHO, had to abandon its studies because China barred access to the lab or its data.

Another hypothesis for the lack of transparency leads us to the desk of Dr. Anthony S. Fauci, the former director of the NIAID (National Institute of Allergy and Infectious Diseases). Fauci has been under fire since it was revealed that the NIAID funded gain-of-function research itself at the Wuhan lab. He defended the decision to fund a study on how to let the genie out of his bottle, saying that it was a necessary step in the development of an antidote.[5]

Two surveys, both in April 2023, showed that Americans overwhelmingly believe in the lab leak theory of COVID-19 origins. Quinnipiac University found that by 64 percent to 22 percent, Americans believed the virus was leaked from the Wuhan lab. The *Economist* / YouGov came to the same conclusion, finding agreement with the lab leak theory ran from 66 percent to 16 percent.[6]

So let's ask the ultimate question: If the evidence pointed to Chinese culpability in originating and leaking the virus and then in covering up its role, what did President Joseph Biden do to hold Beijing accountable for the deaths of a million Americans?

Not much.

On March 23, 2023, Biden issued an executive order directing the intelligence community to use "every tool at its disposal to investigate the origin of COVID." A bit late.[7]

Meanwhile, Biden's own FBI director, Christopher Wray, endorsed the theory that the pandemic was the result of a lab leak in China. The *Guardian* newspaper noted, "The theory that the pandemic originated from a lab leak implied greater Chinese culpability in causing the global health disaster and covering up its role. The administration's position has been that there is no consensus on Covid's beginnings, but (FBI Director) Wray told Fox News: 'The FBI has for quite some time now assessed that the origins of the pandemic are most likely a potential lab incident in Wuhan.'"[8]

If the Wuhan lab leak was accidental, it must rank as one of the great tragedies of humanity. But if it was a deliberate release of the virus—perhaps to stop the Trump reelection and save China's economy—it is one of the worst war crimes in human history.

But Biden's studied inactivity and refusal to condemn even China's failure to cooperate in investigating its origin certainly raises suspicions that he is covering for his patron—the People's Republic of China.

The more pressing question is, What was China doing experimenting with gain-of-function research in the first place?

Whether the leak was accidental or not, people must demand that China be held accountable for experimenting with such a deadly virus.

And now, Biden has affirmed his support of gain-of-function research—the very work that led to the mutation of the COVID-19 virus in the first place.[9]

The media endorsed the decision by a panel of federal advisers to the National Institute of Health on January 27, 2013, to continue to fund the gain-of-function research. They sought to portray it as advancing "a set of proposals to bolster government oversight of pathogen research that could make viruses more transmissible."[10]

Some scientists even balked at the new oversight rules, saying that it might "accidentally hinder gain of function research."[11]

Government advisers said their decision to fund the continued gain-of-function research was necessary because the virus constantly mutates, and finding ways to counter it is like shooting at a moving target.

NIH advisers largely defended the recommendations, arguing that "the idea was not to ban any kind of research, but to—if there are concerns identified—find ways to mitigate them," said Dennis Metzger, professor emeritus in immunology and microbial disease at Albany Medical College.[12]

So we see the medical/research establishment at its very worst, coming together to defend further research—and funding for the research—even at the risk of infecting mankind once again.

All this reminds me of Victor Frankenstein, so proud of his creation that he could not see its evil consequences for humans.

CHAPTER 16

DISMANTLING THE DOLLAR, BRICS BY BRICS

A FEW DECADES FROM now, what will historians say is the most enduring harm Biden inflicted on his country?

Inflation? No, it comes a goes over the years.

Crime? Unless you are a victim, it is just a statistic.

Illegal immigration? By then, Trump will have come back and shut it down.

None of the above. His greatest harm will have been to let the American dollar lose its preeminence in the world and no longer enjoy its status as the global currency.

Should Biden's policies continue to lead us down this road, it will mean the close of the era of American ascendency in the world. The dates on its gravestone will read, "1945–2024."

If we lose our privileged perch atop the global financial system, we will suffer mightily from the loss.

Right now, the US government, unique among all the nations of the world, can simply print all the money that it wants or needs. No checks or balances or even any questions are needed.

When another nation runs a deficit and needs to borrow to make its books balance, it must first convert its currency into dollars on the world market. It cannot just run its printing press and churn out more of its own currency without incurring incredible inflation and finding that its money no longer buys anything around the world. Only the US can print money and be confident of its acceptance everywhere.

Today, we spend about $6.5 trillion a year and take in only $5 trillion in revenues. With the ability to print our own currency, we can bridge the deficit. But without that power, we would have to make huge cuts in our spending, slicing social security, Medicare, Medicaid, and all other programs back to nearly approximate our tax revenues. But the main consequence would be to force us to cut our defense budget, giving China military superiority.[1]

Is it to force a reduction in our defense spending that China is leading the effort to dethrone the dollar?

We earned the right to be the global currency after World War II. At the war's end, the US was the only country left standing. Whether they won or lost, every other country depended on America.

Back then,[2] we produced half of the world's GDP (now we are down to 15 percent).[3] We had the only significant foreign currency reserves. And alone among all nations, we were thriving economically.

At the Bretton Woods Conference in 1944, the dollar formally became the global currency.[4]

In that role, we nursed the world back to health, beginning with our allies in Europe and our former enemies in Germany and Japan. We largely funded the free world in its opposition to communism and led much of the third world out of absolute poverty.

But Biden abused our power to print money to the point where we may be on the verge of losing it.

Until Obama, our budget deficits, while a national problem and political issue, were comparatively minor.

In the late 1990s, under Clinton, our budget was balanced. We had no deficit.

Under Bush, in 2003 and 2004, responding to the increased military spending after 9/11, we ran an annual deficit of about $400 billion. In 2009 following the world economic (subprime) crisis, our deficit soared up to $1.4 trillion, as the Federal Reserve System, under Bush and then Obama, frantically printed money to stop the financial meltdown from pushing the whole economy over the cliff.

From 2009 to 2012, the hangover from the crisis persisted, and it was not until 2013 that the deficit dipped below a trillion dollars ($700 billion). It continued to be relatively under control during the Trump administration, as the deficit stayed below a trillion. In 2017, it was $665 billion; in 2018, it reached $779 billion; and in 2019, it rose to $984 billion.

Then, of course, all went to hell, as COVID-19 struck, and Trump and Congress acted together, swiftly and well, to cushion the economic shock of the national lockdown. In 2020, the deficit went up to $3.1 trillion.

But by the year's end, as Biden took office, businesses reopened, and tax revenues again began to flow. This was where America went wrong.

Biden should have reduced the deficit now that the emergency had passed, but instead, he used his majority in Congress to continue to spend massively. Even though the worst of the COVID-19 pandemic was behind us, the deficit still was $2.8 trillion.

Had Biden ratcheted back spending gradually, we would never have faced the inflation and loss of faith in the dollar we do today. Our credibility as the world's benchmark currency would have stayed intact.

But Biden and the Democrats couldn't help themselves. They had a unique opportunity to raise the federal baseline spending, citing the pandemic as their excuse, passing out hundreds of billions of stimulus checks, and starting all kinds of new programs to buy votes.

The massive stimulus this spending injected into the economy, coming at a time when it was bouncing back, created far too much consumer demand, and the cramped supply chains found that they couldn't keep up with that demand. Major inflation ensued, after very low inflation for the previous forty years.

With each uptick in prices, the dollar lost more of its value, losing a quarter of it from 2017 to 2023.[5]

The world got nervous. Particularly the Arabs did not want to part with their precious oil for dollars that were becoming worth less and less.

So the Organization of the Petroleum Exporting Countries (OPEC) began to demand payment in gold, which had retained most of its value.

Michael Wilkerson of Wall Street's Stormwall Advisors puts the deficit/dollar crisis in perspective: "We are on the verge of a debt and deficit fueled inflationary crisis, one in which our trading and investment counterparts lose all faith and confidence in our government and our currency, and price stability goes out the window."[6]

He quotes economist Peter Bernholz, who wrote in his book *Monetary Regimes and Inflation: History, Economic and Political Relationships* that all recorded high inflation and hyperinflation are linked to unsustainable budget deficits. When the government prints money to pay for its deficit spending, as the US has done for years now, inflation is sure to follow, albeit often at a lag of several years. "Initially," he writes, "runaway deficit spending can be economically stimulative, as we saw last year, but if moderate inflation turns into high inflation, the economy will slow dramatically."[7]

Then things got worse when Russia invaded Ukraine and the United States imposed a global embargo on Moscow.[8] Nobody could do business with Russia in dollars—and nobody wanted to do it in rubles—so gold became the medium of exchange for Russia and the nations that traded with it.

As the embargo forced Russia to stop using dollars and switch to gold, Moscow decided to band together with China to turn away from the dollar entirely as the global currency.

China saw the weakness of the dollar and pounced.

In 2010, the leaders of Brazil, India, and South Africa joined with Russia and China to form the international group that became known as BRICS (Brazil, Russia, India, China, and South Africa).[9] As the dollar fell at the end of the decade, the countries came to modify their trade with one another to eliminate dollars and trade instead either in their local currencies or, more and more, in gold.

The BRICS countries together have 41 percent of the world population, 24 percent of the world GDP, and over 16 percent share in the world trade.[10]

In August 2023, Iran, Saudi Arabia, Argentina, Ethiopia, the UAE, and Egypt joined the BRICS bloc.

Couching their association in nonpolitical terms, the BRICS countries made no secret of their desire to escape from under American hegemony.

Wilkerson has repeatedly warned that financial sanctions are a form of economic warfare that would not only be ineffective against Russia as a target but also boomerang back to the US and the West. He asserts that sanctions are already pushing the BRICS and other countries to turn away from the dollar, knowing that what happened to Russia could easily happen to them.

It was not so bad that the US government stopped Americans from doing business in Russia. But it also pursued what it called "secondary sanctions," punishing third parties that did business with Russia.

Wilkerson argues that "secondary sanctions" would lead the sanctioned countries and companies to abandon the dollar entirely and do their trading in local currencies or gold.

Ryan Berg, director of the Americas Program at the US-based Center for Strategic and International Studies (CSIS), pointed out that "Russia's invasion of Ukraine has made the BRICS more relevant, especially for countries in the Global South that want to resist the West's 'autocracy-vs.-democracy' narrative."[11]

China has taken aim at the United States' relationship with Saudi Arabia, the third largest oil producer after the US and Russia.

Ironically, it was the Saudi monarchy that catalyzed the US dollar's role as the global currency back in 1945.

Ailing and soon to die at that time, Franklin D. Roosevelt visited the kingdom as he came home from the Yalta Conference in 1945. The purpose of this physically taxing journey was to cement the Saudi commitment to sell oil only for US dollars, a deal that may now be ending during the Biden administration.

Saudi Arabia put the nail in the deal FDR negotiated with the House of Saud by joining BRICS and renouncing the dollar.

The arrangement came as "Saudi Arabia also significantly strengthened its energy ties with China by announcing on Monday a $3.6 billion deal to buy 10% of China's Rongsheng Petrochemical, which would see it supply 480,000 barrels per day of crude oil to the company."[12]

The collapse of US-Saudi relations can be laid at the doorstep of Joe Biden, whose anti–fossil fuel policies and antagonistic attitude toward Saudi Arabia have led to the current rift.

Talk of dedollarization is increasingly rife, and under pressure from Russia, the BRICS countries are now developing a new currency to replace the US dollar.

Brazil's leftist president Luiz Inácio Lula da Silva ("Lula") chimed in. "Every night," he said, he asks himself "why all countries have to base their trade on the dollar."[13]

Joseph W. Sullivan, a senior adviser at the Lindsey Group and a former special adviser and staff economist at the White House Council of Economic Advisers during the Trump administration, said, "A BRICS-issued currency would be different. It'd be like a new union of up-and-coming discontents who, on the scale of GDP, now collectively outweigh not only the reigning hegemon, the United States, but the entire G-7 weight class put together."[14]

TFI Global News writes, "It looks like Biden's administrative playbook to counter the rise of BRICS is more or less a joke. . . . The US administration is looking for alternatives to replace Russian energy amid the Ukraine war. . . . The US has long been trying to influence the Middle Eastern nations to increase their output and help Europe. Biden recently visited the Middle East and tried to pressure the Saudi leadership to take an anti-Russia stance. He wanted to break up the OPEC+ alliance between Saudi Arabia and Russia so that the US could exert control on the energy supplies in the region."[15]

However, Mohammed bin Salman, the crown prince of Saudi Arabia, spoke with President Putin during the week of Biden's visit and discussed further expansion of trade and economic cooperation and significantly also underscored "the importance of further coordination within OPEC+. Biden's actions have triggered the rise of an Eastern bloc against the West."[16]

Now the European Commission has publicly welcomed the end of the American petrodollar, heralding what they describe as a new "multipolar global currency regime." The EU says that it would like to see its euro currency adopted for more international energy transactions soon. "The Commission will continue promoting the international role of the euro and, more generally, is supportive of a multipolar global currency regime."[17]

On July 8, 2023, Reuters ran a story that said that the BRICS countries are planning to issue a joint currency backed by gold. Reuters said that the currency will be announced in August 2023 at the BRICS summit in Johannesburg, South Africa. It did not happen in Johannesburg as predicted, but it definitely will in the very near future!

Such a currency would be a giant step toward ending the dollar's supremacy. After all, if you have a choice between a currency backed by the say-so of the US government and one backed by gold, you would be a fool to stay with the dollar.

Biden fails to grasp that "with Middle Eastern energy-rich countries looking to join the BRICS alliance, the grouping could become stronger than ever with all partners bringing in necessary resources."[18]

Meanwhile, Biden's domestic economic policies almost seem to be designed to undermine the dollar. By massive borrowing and spending, he is weakening the dollar's credibility, and by refusing to cut spending, even as the US teeters on the brink of a global default, he hastens the dollar's demise.

Indeed, Fitch, the global firm that evaluates the financial stability of the world's countries, has just knocked the US down a
notch, perhaps the beginning of the end for the dollar.[19]

With Joe Biden, we are always forced to choose whether
his policies are stupid or designed to hurt the United States of
America and to benefit his patron, China. The demise of the
dollar—hastened by Biden—poses just such a conundrum.

CHAPTER 17

RESEARCH AND DEVELOPMENT CHINA STYLE—STEAL IT

WHEN JAPAN EMERGED AS a challenger to America's lead on the global economic playing field, all agreed that it earned its second-place ranking by doing its own research and development and mastering the art of miniaturizing new technologies. But as China has eclipsed Japan and closed in on the US for the top spot, their MO is very different: they don't invent it; they steal it.

Like the sirens that tried to lure Ulysses to his death on the rocks, China's supposedly "untapped" market of 1.4 billion consumers is a siren song luring American companies to China and to their deaths.

American companies move to China, where their trademarked and patented intellectual property, their trade secrets, their technology, and their competitive edge are all first stolen, then copied, and finally replaced by Chinese companies.

And yet America's top companies fall for the trick time after time. It amounts to massive assisted corporate suicide.

When an American company wants to relocate to China, it must first acquire a Chinese partner. But in this forced marriage, the American firm must be the minority stakeholder and give 51 percent of their shares to their Chinese "partner."

As Navarro writes, giving the Chinese firm majority rights "means loss of direct control of the enterprise by the American company. More subtly, this condition gives the Chinese majority partner—most often a state-controlled enterprise—the power to access all information about the venture, including trade secrets."[1]

But China makes the requirement that the American company commit suicide even more explicit. Navarro explains how the Chinese require "forced technology transfer. To wit, American companies must surrender their intellectual property to their Chinese partners as a condition of market entry. The practical effect of this condition is to facilitate the dissemination of various technologies not just to the Chinese partner directly involved but also to the Chinese government and to other potential Chinese competitors. By surrendering to this condition, Western companies, in effect, create their own Chinese competitors virtually overnight."[2]

Finally, China requires the relocation of corporate research and development to China's shores, away from the US: "Once an American company surrenders its autonomy," Navarro warns, "it is only a matter of time before the Chinese companies digest these technologies and use them to outcompete the American company—not just on Chinese soil but in the global marketplace."[3]

The Westinghouse Electric Corporation exemplified this tendency toward corporate suicide when it handed over to China "more than 75,000 documents as the initial part of the technology transfer deal" it cut with Beijing, hoping to access the vast market for nuclear power plant construction in China.[4]

Westinghouse, like many American companies, failed to appreciate the insight of President John F. Kennedy in his inaugural address that "those who foolishly sought power by riding the back of the tiger ended up inside."[5]

In another example of assisted corporate suicide, the *Wall Street Journal* reports that "when the Japanese and European companies that pioneered the high-speed rail agreed to build trains for China, they thought they'd be getting access to a booming new market. . . . What they didn't count on was having to compete with Chinese firms who adapted their technology and turned it against them just a few years later."[6]

John Gapper, writing in the *Financial Times*, describes how "a foreign company [first] cedes its intellectual property to a Chinese State-Owned Enterprise (SOE). Then, they are squeezed to the margins of China's domestic market" and must face a Chinese competitor armed with their technology.

Gapper sums it up well: "China wants to use its market power to take a shortcut by digesting others' intellectual property."[7] But Biden does nothing to rein in China's theft of our technology. He should fine American companies that move to China and surrender the intellectual property they developed while they were still in the US. They should suffer tax penalties.

But we all know that Biden will not bite the hand that feeds him and his voracious family.

By stealing technology from an established American company that wants to locate in China, Beijing can acquire a certain amount of global power. But what about the real heart of American know-how, the small entrepreneur who, alone or with a few friends in his basement, comes up with a world-changing innovation?

How do you compete with that?

Answer: you stifle it in its cradle.

CHAPTER 18

BIDEN STRANGLES THE
US PATENT PROTECTIONS

LEGALLY, INTELLECTUAL PROPERTY IS protected by patents and copyrights that restrict when competitors can use what you have developed. But under the Biden administration, the US Patent Office has so watered down these protections that they do little, practically, to deter or punish Chinese theft of American technology.

In China's efforts to pirate our technology, they find allies in big-tech American companies like Google, Facebook, Apple, and Amazon who are also working to stifle new American science, technology, and invention. Why? Because they don't control it and are scared to death that somebody will invent something better than they have and send them spiraling into the dustbin of history.

In fact, the US high-tech industry realizes that most major innovation comes not from corporate behemoths like themselves but from small inventors toiling away in obscurity in their garages. So it uses the patent system not to encourage or protect innovation but to strangle it in its infancy.

China is cheering big tech on, hoping to slow the pace of American technological innovation. If it succeeds, China can gain a big advantage.

How can the tech giants—in the US and China—stifle innovation? They can't dull the human brain. Or human energy and creativity. People will still have good new ideas. Nor can they dry up venture capital. If there are good ideas that can make money, there will be investors to put up the cash.

But there is one sweet spot they can hit that will do the trick: they can eviscerate the patent system. If thieves, phonies, and impostors—or just big companies—can steal your ideas and swipe your inventions, you'll stop coming up with them, and your backers won't fund you. You'll have to heed the advice of your mothers and get a real job.

Your protection, as an inventor or an innovator, is the US patent system, which shields your invention so nobody can steal it. It also lets you publish what you've come up with—once it's patent protected—so others can take your creativity one step further, building on your progress.

Under the Trump administration, the US Patent and Trademark Office was run by Andrei Iancu, a Romanian American engineer and expert on intellectual property (IP). Iancu moved aggressively to stop big tech in the US and China from stifling American innovation. But with Trump and Iancu gone, the rules have changed, and there is little real protection against theft of intellectual property.[1]

The favorite tactic of big American companies and their Chinese allies is to use the very system erected to stop the theft of IP to enable it. The tech giants keep close track of new inventions, and when the inventor files for a patent to protect what he has created, big tech sues through the patent system to block it.[2]

At the very least, the litigation they bring makes the inventor spend a ton of money on courts and lawyers to defend his patent, and he may even lose and find his patent thrown out.

This strategy works well and often overwhelms the new inventors with legal costs. Often just kids in a garage, new inventors are often chronically short of capital as they shop their inventions around, hoping for investors.

Once a patent is denied or the investor runs out of cash to defend it, all his competitor—domestic or Chinese—needs is a smart phone to photograph the new designs and appropriate them for himself.

Sometimes, however, the patent for an innovation has already been issued, making it impossible to steal the plans. The thieves can try to get the patent thrown out, but the history of these lawsuits isn't very good—70 percent lost. Not very good odds. So big tech changed the system to make it easier to steal.

Google, Facebook, Amazon, and Apple got the patent office, under Obama, to hire new judges who'd play ball with them. In fact, they got a whole new court with its own rules and its own new judges.

They spent millions on lobbyists to get Congress to pass one of those laws that say they do the exact opposite of what they really do. The bill was the Leahy-Smith America Invents Act (AIA).[3] Its hidden purpose was to make sure that America didn't invent much of anything at all.

The AIA lets a big tech company that is accused of infringing on a patent challenge the patent not in court before newly created administrative judges, many of whom are hand-picked to do big tech's bidding and that of their Chinese allies.[4]

And until recently, the law allowed tech companies to challenge the same patent repeatedly until it won or the inventor ran out of money. This way, big tech companies were able to copy a patent and get away with it, never having to face a judge or jury.

But when President Trump appointed Andrei Iancu to run the Patent and Trademark Office, he instituted new rules to make sure that those who infringed on patents could no longer harass the original inventor.[5]

He stopped big tech from bringing unlimited challenges to new patents to bankrupt the new inventor with legal fees. Once you sued to block a patent and lost, you couldn't come back for a second bite at the apple.

But when Biden took over, he repealed the Trump rule and allowed big tech and their Chinese allies to drown inventors in repeat lawsuits.[6]

Why did Biden play ball? Remember how Biden got elected—he got big tech to muzzle Trump during the campaign. They had, after all, helped Biden bury the story about Hunter's laptop that showed how Joe Biden was working with Hunter to help the corrupt energy company in Ukraine—Burisma—and implied that he was sharing in the payments Hunter was getting from the Chinese.[7] The new regulations tying down the patenting process were their payback.

So now, under Biden, American inventors are getting the point: the patent system offers little protection. The value of the average patent on the open market dropped by 60 percent, and the number of patent sales is down by two-thirds. Big tech, with Biden's help, is stomping on innovation, particularly in the areas of artificial intelligence and 5G.

Before Trump, the US ranked twelfth among all developed countries in the strength of its patent protections. Trump and Andrei Iancu brought it back up to number two in the world. Now big tech is reversing all that progress.

Venture capital investors have stopped funding inventions but are now putting their money into social networking and consumer finance. No patents needed there.

CHAPTER 19

CHINA STEALS OUR INVENTIONS

THE PATENT OFFICE ISN'T the only problem China, with Biden's assistance, is putting in the path of the American innovator.

Like salmon dodging bears as they swim upstream to roost, the small inventor no sooner makes it past big tech than it runs into Chinese espionage. China's MO is to steal American IP, replicate it, and then replace the US company both in the Chinese domestic market and around the world.

FBI director Christopher Wray says that the modern Chinese industrial espionage apparatus—in its organization, scope, and ambition—far eclipses its predecessors: "We consistently see that it's the Chinese government that poses the biggest long-term threat to our economic and national security."[1]

Since the 1990s, US prosecutors have charged more than seven hundred people with espionage, IP theft, illegally exporting military technology, and other crimes linked to China. Two-thirds of the cases have led to convictions, and most of the rest are pending or involve fugitives.

Bloomberg reports that the Chinese intelligence-gathering apparatus relies not only on trained spies and officers of China's Ministry of State Security but also on ordinary engineers and scientists.[2]

This machinery remains largely opaque to outsiders. US authorities have tended to focus mainly on those who spy on us and feed information to their handlers in China. By going after individual spies, US authorities have been like narcotic investigators pursuing low-level dealers while the larger criminal infrastructure hums along unscathed.

One of the biggest culprits in industrial espionage is Huawei, a prominent Chinese tech company and chip maker.

When the Trump administration busted Meng Wanzhou, a senior Huawei executive and the daughter of the company's founder, it exposed how Chinese intel operated to steal our innovations.

Huawei's efforts to steal our IP went far. Federal prosecutors charged that "Huawei recruited employees of competitors to steal intellectual property. The company also provided incentives to its own employees by offering bonuses to those who brought in the most valuable stolen information, and it used proxies, including professors at research institutions, in the pursuit of inside information."[3]

The stolen information included antenna- and robot-testing technology as well as user manuals for internet routers. "One goal of the theft," the Justice Department said, "was to allow Huawei to save on research and development costs."[4]

The indictment detailed many examples of industrial theft by Huawei, some of them almost comically brazen.

In one May 2013 episode, according to the Meng indictment, a Huawei engineer removed a robotic arm from the laboratory of a rival company based in Washington State, stashing it in a laptop bag.[5] The engineer emailed photographs and measurements of the arm to others at Huawei before the arm was returned to the Washington company, which had discovered the theft.

At a 2004 trade show in Chicago, a Huawei employee was found in the middle of the night in the booth of a technology company "removing the cover from a networking device and taking photographs of the circuitry inside," prosecutors said.[6] The employee wore a badge that listed his employer as "Weihua," or Huawei spelled with its syllables reversed.

But it has occurred to China, Why spend all your time and money copying American technology? Steal it at its source: in American colleges and universities.

CHAPTER 20

CHINA FUNDS OUR COLLEGES AND UNIVERSITIES TO TRY TO CONTROL THEM

BEIJING DISCOVERED EARLY IN its global battle for power that American institutions of higher learning always have their hands out for money. By giving to these colleges and universities, China scores a twofer.

First, it gets to spy on, capture, pirate, and replicate the best fruits of American science and technology. And second, it gets to influence the future leaders of America on the campuses where they incubate.

China acquires influence at US colleges and universities through both the tuition its students pay and the billions of grant money Beijing gives American universities.

The overall number of Chinese students at US higher education institutions has nearly tripled over the past decade, from

130,000 in 2009 to 370,000 in 2020. China is the largest foreign source of students at US colleges and universities.

The House Committee on Foreign Affairs documents the extent of Chinese inroads: "The PRC [People's Republic of China] is the largest source of foreign donations to U.S. universities since 2013. The tuition paid by Chinese students is worth an estimated $12 billion per year. Chinese sources have participated in donations or contracts worth more than $426 million to U.S. universities since 2011."[1]

China sets up think tanks in American universities—and even in elementary, middle, and high schools, called Confucius Institutes (CIs).

The House Committee on Foreign Affairs reports, "In the last 15 years, the Chinese government has opened more than 100 CIs in the United States. Confucius classrooms are currently in more than 500 elementary, middle, and high schools in the United States."[2]

The FBI reports, "CIs are ultimately beholden to the Chinese government. . . . CI funding can include conditions that limit a school's autonomy by censuring political debate and preventing discussions on certain topics, such as Taiwan and Tibet."[3]

China's Thousand Talents Plan recruits Chinese researchers studying in the US to focus on cutting-edge technology in American universities. At the very least, these researchers can gain access to fundamental research, but the House Committee warns, "Chinese researchers with connections to the People's Liberation Army and blacklisted Chinese companies have been given licenses by the Department of Commerce to work on controlled technology."[4]

The influx of Chinese money to our institutions of higher education has been massive. In just a six-month period, from January to June 2021, "interests based in China contributed over $168 million to 46 American colleges and universities, according to data compiled by *The College Fix*."[5]

The Department of Education Foreign Gift Reporting database lists over five thousand donations from China to US institutions of higher education since 1987. The donations were made in the form of contracts and "restricted gifts" and totaled almost $3 billion.

The University of California, Los Angeles, for example, got a single $60 million contract in 2018, and the University of California received $211 million in total, making it one of the largest cumulative recipients of Chinese cash. The University of Illinois has collected over $87.5 million in contributions from Chinese sources. The university operates a joint campus with Zhejiang University in Heijang, China, and accepted two individual donations of $19.5 million each! Behind UCLA and Illinois was the Massachusetts Institute of Technology, which accepted eighty-five gifts and contracts totaling over $86.5 million.[6]

China bestowed special largesse on America's Ivy League campuses. Harvard University accepted 158 gifts and contracts worth over $217 million, and Columbia University collected 232 gifts and contracts worth nearly $100 million.

The Higher Education Act of 1965 requires institutes of higher education to report any foreign gifts of more than $250,000.

But the US Department of Education's 2020 report, quoted in College Fix, claims several large universities received billions

of dollars in assets "using an assortment of related interme-
diaries, including functionally captive foundations, foreign
operating units, and other structures."[7]

In 2020, the US Department of Education found $6.5 bil-
lion in previously unreported foreign money.

And the Chinese investment in US higher education is yield-
ing results for Beijing. Whether in US or Chinese universities,
Navarro reports that "China is producing ten or more times the
number of scientists and engineers as the United States." He
warns, "We, as a country, are falling far behind in these fields."[8]

Of course, none of these gifts to American colleges and universities offer the return on investment to China that the more
than $60 million that it reportedly gave the University of Penn-
sylvania, notably to the Penn Biden Center.

While the president may worry—in public—about China's
penetration of our higher education system, he himself has been
its number one beneficiary.

CHAPTER 21

CHINA USES STUDENTS TO SPY ON US DEFENSE INDUSTRIES

CHINA IS USING ITS vast army of students studying in the United States, expatriate scientists, and businesspeople to gather intel. The more than 350,000 students from China who study in the US every year are a fertile source of new spies.

CNN reports, "The sheer size of the Chinese student population at US universities presents a major challenge for law enforcement and intelligence agencies tasked with striking the necessary balance between protecting America's open academic environment and mitigating the risk to national security."[1]

Colleges and universities have become soft targets for Chinese intel operatives. Rather than going to the expense of having trained spies attempt to infiltrate US universities and businesses, Joe Augustyn, a former CIA officer, says, "Chinese intelligence services have strategically utilized members of its student popu-lation to act as 'access agents' or 'covert influencers.'"[2]

"We allow 350,000 or so Chinese students here every year," William Evanina, director of the National Counterintelligence and Security Center, said in April 2018 during an Aspen Insti-tute conference. "That's a lot. We have a very liberal visa policy for them. Ninety-nine point nine percent of those students are here legitimately and doing great research and helping the global trade and economy. But it is a tool that is used by the Chinese govern-ment to facilitate nefarious activity here in the US."[3]

China wants to use its US-based students to compress the time it takes to acquire certain technological capabilities.

A senior official in the Office of the Director of National Intelligence notes that the close contact between Chinese and American students at US universities makes espionage easier: "In a world where we are training their scientists and engineers, and their scientists and engineers were already good on their own, we are just making them able to not have to toil for the same amount of time to get capabilities that will rival or test us."[4]

China pushes back on charges that it uses its exchange stu-dents as spies. "Such statements are completely untrue and made with ulterior motives. People-to-people exchanges form a basis for the promotion of China-US cooperation in all areas, which is in the common interest of both peoples," China's Min-istry of Foreign Affairs told CNN in a statement.[5]

It's hard to weed out the spies from the students. Augustyn points out that Chinese students "don't just come here to spy . . . they come here to study and a lot of it is legitimate. But there is no question in my mind, depending on where they are and what they are doing, that they have a role to play for their government. . . . We know without a doubt that anytime a graduate student from China comes to the US, they are briefed when they go, and debriefed when they come back."[6]

For example, the US arrested and prosecuted a student who arrived in Chicago in August 2013 and in December 2013 was "approached by a Chinese intelligence officer who, initially at least, used a false identity," according to FBI Special Agent Andrew McKay.[7]

Like thousands of Chinese nationals who come to the US each year, the foreign student, Ji Chaoqun, entered the country on an F-1 visa to study electrical engineering at the Illinois Institute of Technology, where he ultimately earned a master's degree.

"Then," CNN reports, "Ji was approached by a high-level Chinese intelligence official, who presented himself as a professor at Nanjing University of Aeronautics and Astronautics. Ji would funnel him background reports on other Chinese civilians living in the US who might be pressured to serve as spies—in this case, in the strategically critical US industries of aerospace and technology. And he would lie to US officials about it, according to the complaint filed by FBI investigators."[8]

In the complaint, FBI agents said they discovered thirty-six text messages on one iCloud account that Ji and the intelligence officer allegedly exchanged between December 2013 and July 2015. In 2016, after he graduated, Ji enlisted in the US Army Reserve under a program in which foreign nationals can be recruited if their skills are considered "vital to the national interest."[9]

Ji's case has been linked to the indictment of a Chinese intelligence officer named Xu Yanjun, who "was arrested in Belgium for allegedly stealing trade secrets from US aerospace companies. He is the first Chinese intelligence officer to be extradited for prosecution in the US."[10]

FBI director Christopher Wray told a Senate Intelligence Committee hearing that China is "exploiting the very open research and development environment that we have."[11]

But Wray sees progress in his counterintel operations: "One of the things that I've been most encouraged about in an otherwise bleak landscape is the degree to which American companies are waking up, American universities are waking up, our foreign partners are waking up."[12]

"Sen. Mark Warner of Virginia, the leading Democrat on the Senate's Select Committee on Intelligence, stressed that it is important to recognize 'that the Chinese government has enormous power over its citizens. . . . In China, only the government can grant someone permission to leave the country,'" and the Chinese government—in some cases—uses its power over its citizens to "'encourage those citizens to commit acts of scientific or industrial espionage to the benefit of the Chinese government.'"[13]

CHAPTER 22

BIDEN ABOLISHES THE PROGRAM TO FIGHT CHINESE ESPIONAGE

BUT DESPITE THIS GAPING intelligence leak, the Biden Justice Department announced on February 23, 2022, that it is shutting down a program initiated during the Trump administration to counter Chinese espionage, saying it amounts to racial profiling.

Politico reports, "The three-year-old effort, known as the China Initiative, was being cast aside largely because of perceptions that it unfairly painted Chinese Americans and U.S. residents of Chinese origin as disloyal."[1]

"By grouping cases under the China Initiative rubric, we helped give rise to a harmful perception that the department applies a lower standard to investigate and prosecute criminal conduct related to that country or that we in some way view people with racial, ethnic or familial ties to China differently," said assistant attorney general for national security Matthew Olsen.[2]

Olsen said department officials had concluded that the enforcement program singling out China was ill-advised and better reframed as part of a more wide-ranging effort to counter threats posed by Russia, Iran, and other countries. "I'm convinced that we need a broader approach, one that looks across all of these threats and uses all of our authorities to combat them," he said.[3]

Olsen said he met with a variety of Asian American groups who have complained about the program and agreed with them that the effort was in some ways harming US national security by discouraging skilled experts of Chinese origin from pursuing their work in the US.[4]

How convenient for China—and for Joe Biden and his family—that the Biden administration has stopped focusing on the Chinese students studying in the US as possible spies.

And the White House is dead set against congressional efforts to expose China's theft of our technology.

Republicans sought to amend the 2024 National Defense Authorization Act (NDAA) to force the Pentagon to disclose information about foreign nationals working on military-funded research programs at American universities, where Chinese spies are known to steal proprietary research. Biden is doing all he can to slam the door on these disclosure requirements. He does not want Americans to see so vividly the immense returns China has garnered from its payments to Biden.

Wise to the way China is co-opting our technology and making off with our secrets, Indiana Republican congressman Jim Banks—the author of the China disclosure amendment—is pushing hard to increase pressure on American universities that partner with the CCP on sensitive research projects.

Under Banks's amendment, the Pentagon would have to publicly disclose the identities of all individuals working on government-funded projects, including the "date and place of birth, country of citizenship, and immigration status in the case of a foreign national."[5]

The White House said it "strongly opposes" this measure because it would "impose a significant increase in disclosure requirements for university research funded by DoD."[6]

The White House also expressed concerns the reporting requirements could "jeopardize the Department's ability to fund universities in States with nondiscrimination laws that prohibit citizenship and nationality reporting." The administration also worries the strict parameters would "deter the ability to attract the best and brightest foreign scientists from working with the Department."[7] How far will Biden go to protect the spying of his Chinese handlers and forestall American efforts to deter them?

CHAPTER 23

BIDEN LETS FENTANYL FROM CHINA FLOW ACROSS OUR BORDERS

THE LEADING CAUSE OF death for America's youth is fentanyl abuse. In 2021, over a hundred thousand Americans died from drug overdose, two-thirds of it from fentanyl.

Most of the fentanyl is mass-produced in Mexico using chemicals from China before being pressed into pills.

The Republican amendment to the defense appropriations bill—opposed by Biden—would order the secretary of defense to determine whether Chinese government officials assisted or were aware of the transportation of fentanyl precursors to Mexican drug cartels.

Congressman Jim Banks (R-IN), the author of the amendment, said, "The Chinese Communist Party is poisoning and killing nearly a hundred thousand Americans each year with 'Made in China' fentanyl while their spies infiltrate our universities and even high-level government laboratories. . . . It's an upside-down world in the Biden White House, where appeasing Communist China comes first, and America's national security and well-being comes last."[1]

The *Free Beacon* reports that "Banks's fentanyl measure also attracted White House opposition, primarily because it would force the Pentagon to publicly acknowledge that China is pumping deadly drugs into America—an accusation that could inflame tensions at a time when American diplomats are trying to repair relations with Beijing."[2]

The newspaper reports that Biden's ambassador to China, for instance, "recently said that the Chinese Communist Party is not responsible for America's fentanyl crisis, even though virtually all of the ingredients for the drug are produced in China and shipped to Mexican cartels illicitly running the drug into the country."

The White House says any effort to tie China to the fentanyl crisis would interfere with its ability to "ensure foreign assistance or engagement is carried out in a manner consistent with foreign policy priorities."[3]

Is that the real problem, or is it that exposing Biden's coddling of China while it pours drugs into America's kids could offend Beijing's friend in the White House?

CHAPTER 24

CHINA DEVELOPS A MONOPOLY OF RARE EARTH MINERALS

NOT ONLY DOES THE green revolution hobble the United States in its competition with China, but it specifically lets China develop a stranglehold on the American economy.

Environmental activists and extremists are a core constituency for President Biden. The so-called Green New Deal, launched in 2006 by Representative Alexandria Ocasio-Cortez (D-NY) and Senator Ed Markey (D-MA), calls for 100 percent clean, renewable energy by 2030, financed by a tax on carbon emissions.

Their vision is a bold one. All cars will run on electric batteries. No more gasoline-powered internal combustion engines. All electrical power will be generated by renewable sources like wind and solar and supplemented by traditional renewable sources like hydro and nuclear. No more coal or oil burning. All zoning codes will be overhauled to require the ultimate in energy efficiency, and existing structures will have to be retrofitted for the new technology.

The problem with the vision is that the entire green revolution is made in China.

The electric cars would all be powered by Chinese batteries, as would the wind turbines and solar energy panels. All made in China.[1]

Meanwhile, the Beijing government has refused to commit itself to reducing carbon emissions soon but rather builds a new coal-fired plant every week.

The reason for the Chinese dominance in green technology is, oddly, a product of the very environmental movement that is its catalyst.

The essential ingredients that make batteries work are rare earth minerals. They are a group of fifteen elements in the periodic table known as the lanthanide series. Rare earth minerals are categorized into light (lanthanum to samarium) and heavy (europium to lutetium). The latter are less common and consequently more expensive.

Before the 1980s, the United States was the world's foremost producer of rare earth minerals such as neodymium, lanthanum, yttrium, cerium, terbium, dysprosium, praseodymium, scandium, lutetium, and eight more equally unpronounceable names. These tongue twisters are vital to operating our computers, television remotes, GPS systems, and computer batteries.

But since the turn of the millennium, the US has lost its global dominance in rare earth minerals to China, which now produces 80 percent of them.

The US once was the dominant global supplier of rare earth minerals until the environmental movement closed the mines in California and Nevada that produced much of the world's supply.

We are left with only one operational mine for these essential minerals—in Mountain Pass, California.

Why were the mines closed? Because bureaucrats at the International Atomic Energy Agency (IAEA) decided to expand their jurisdiction to cover the mining, extraction, and processing of rare earth minerals.

It was a crazy decision and a very costly one. Rare earth minerals are not radioactive and, therefore, should not be under IAEA jurisdiction. But they are usually found right next to uranium deposits that are, of course, radioactive. Because of their proximity to uranium, the IAEA decided to regulate rare earth minerals.

The decision required such extensive paperwork and compliance costs that it forced all the existing mines out of business. China, which is not a signatory to the treaties establishing the IAEA, was not bound by the decision and could continue to mine the minerals without having to comply with the agency's strictures.

All the American rare earth extraction teams and experts moved to China, which inherited the American monopoly and today controls the industry.

While there are plans to build more mines and processing facilities—largely initiated by Trump—they will take years to come to fruition.

Felix K. Chang, writing for the Foreign Policy Research Institute, recounts how "a once-shuttered rare earths mine in

California reopened in 2018; new companies, like Rare Element Resources and UCore Rare Metals, have begun to operate in Texas and Alaska respectively. In the meantime, the U.S. Department of Defense awarded Australia's Lynas Rare Earths, the biggest, rare earth metals producer outside of China, a grant to build a light rare earths refinery in Texas."[2]

Trump also ordered the Pentagon to give priority in purchasing rare earth minerals to American sources, and this regulation helped restore part of the US production capacity, but not enough to blunt Chinese domination of the field.

Trump's policies, nevertheless, began to bear fruit. China's share of global rare earth metals production slipped from 80 percent in 2017 to 60 percent in 2021, according to the US Geological Survey.[3]

Meanwhile, with blissful abandon, President Joe Biden has proposed a massive expansion in electric cars, funding five hundred thousand charging stations for their batteries around the country.[4]

But with China controlling the globe's rare earth minerals, if we switch from gas-powered cars to electric cars, we become totally dependent on China.

Instead of Arab sheiks controlling our destiny, Chinese communist apparatchiks would.

The Chinese domination of the field is even more troublesome from a strategic and military point of view. Rare earth minerals are vital to telecommunications, guidance systems, radars, and many military applications.

CHAPTER 25

BIDEN GIVES AWAY OUR RARE EARTH MINERAL MINING TO SAVE A LAKE

BIDEN GAVE IT ALL away.

He blocked mining companies from operating near the Boundary Waters on the Duluth Complex in Minnesota, which the Twin Metals Minnesota mining company says contains about 95 percent of the nation's nickel reserves, 88 percent of the cobalt, 51 percent of the platinum, 48 percent of the palladium, and 34 percent of the nation's copper. Biden banned mining there on these 225,000 acres of federal land for more than twenty years.

Those rare earth minerals are vital for electric vehicle production and lithium-ion batteries. Without domestic rare earth mineral mining, the nation must rely on countries with few labor or environmental laws, such as the Democratic Republic of the Congo, where 75 percent of the supply of cobalt is mined to make lithium-ion batteries and electric vehicles.

Biden's secretary of the interior, Deb Haaland, signed the withdrawal order for 225,504 acres in the Superior National Forest in northeastern Minnesota.

"The Department of the Interior takes seriously our obligations to steward public lands and waters on behalf of all Americans. Protecting a place like Boundary Waters is key to supporting the health of the watershed and its surrounding wildlife, upholding our Tribal trust and treaty responsibilities, and boosting the local recreation economy," Haaland said in a January 2023 statement.[1]

Environmentalist groups welcomed the announcement.

"Today's science-based decision is a massive win for Boundary Waters protection," Becky Rom, national chair of the Campaign to Save the Boundary Waters, said in a statement. "You don't allow America's most toxic industry next to America's most popular Wilderness. The Boundary Waters is a paradise of woods and water. It is an ecological marvel, a world-class outdoor destination, and an economic engine for hundreds of businesses and many thousands of people. This decision moves America ever closer to permanently protecting this beloved Wilderness."[2]

The move will likely shutter the proposed Twin Metals Minnesota mine near Ely. Twin Metals Minnesota said it was "deeply disappointed and stunned" over the decision.

"This region sits on top of one of the world's largest deposits of critical minerals that are vital in meeting our nation's goals to transition to a clean energy future, to create American jobs, to strengthen our national security and to bolster domestic supply chains," the company said in a statement. "We believe our project plays a critical role in addressing all of these priorities, and we remain committed to enforcing Twin Metals' rights."[3]

Minnesota Republican congressman Pete Stauber said the mining ban leaves America reliant on Chinese-owned mines in the Democratic Republic of the Congo. "Not even one month ago, Joe Biden signed an agreement to fund mining projects in Chinese-owned mines in the Congo, where over 40,000 children work as slaves in forced labor and inhumane conditions with no environmental protections," Stauber said in a statement. "Meanwhile today's mining ban nullifies a Project Labor Agreement with the local building and construction trade unions. America needs to develop our vast mineral wealth, right here at home, with high-wage, union protected jobs instead of continuing to send American taxpayer dollars to countries like the Congo that use child slave labor."[4]

All this begs the fundamental question, Did China's deals with the corrupt Biden family have anything to do with Biden's action to ban rare earth mineral production in Minnesota while funding Chinese development in the Congo?

By racing ahead with electric cars and charging stations, Biden is literally putting the cart before the horse—or, if you will, the electric car before the battery.

It has taken America more than fifty years to get free of OPEC's domination. Because of fracking and offshore drilling, we have managed to increase our domestic oil production so much that we are now the largest producer in the world.

But Biden is about to give this all away by moving away from gasoline and toward electric cars before there is an adequate capacity to manufacture batteries in the US.

Indeed, the shortage of manufacturing capacity for batteries lies squarely in the path of almost all of Biden's green agenda and in the way of America's national security.

These batteries, powered by rare earth minerals, are essential to produce solar panels and wind turbines. In thinking he can achieve full self-sufficiency in renewable energy without the necessary expansion of rare earth mineral production and processing, Biden is like an aging and confused Don Quixote tilting at windmills.

Rare earth minerals are also key in the production of smartphones digital cameras, flat-screen TVs, computer hard disks, LED lights, and computer monitors.

In the defense sector, they are necessary components in missile guidance systems, jet engines, satellites, lasers, and night-vision goggles.

We all would like to see electric cars replace the internal combustion engine. That would lessen carbon emissions—about half of which are from cars and trucks—and cut pollution dramatically. But we do not want to do so before we can manufacture their batteries without depending on our main competitor and worst enemy to supply them.

Again, the basic question looms: Did the payments the corrupt Biden family has gotten from China lead to Biden's decision to cripple American rare earth mineral production?

950 million barrels."

CHAPTER 26

BIDEN GIVES AWAY
OUR OIL TO CHINA

ON NOVEMBER 23, 2021, PRESIDENT Joe Biden released
fifty million barrels of oil from the US Strategic Petroleum
Reserve.

But right before the decision to release the oil, on November 19 and 21, US secretary of energy Jennifer Granholm had
two one-on-one conversations with China National Energy
Administration chairman Zhang Jianhua.

The stated goal of the release of oil from our strategic reserve
was to lower energy prices, but according to a statement by
House energy and commerce chairwoman Cathy McMorris
Rodgers, a Republican from Washington, and then representative Fred Upton, a Republican from Michigan, China will
receive a significant portion of the oil released from the Strategic Petroleum Reserve.

They wrote, "China ramped up its purchases of crude oil from Russia and the United States to boost its own reserves, even as oil prices surged and President Biden called for a coordinated release. As a result, China may now control the world's largest stockpile of oil, with total crude inventories estimated at 950 million barrels."[1]

CHAPTER 27

BIDEN HELPS CHINA'S MIND-CONTROL PROJECTS

IN SEPTEMBER 2021, SHORTLY after taking office, President Biden's administration decided to free Meng Wanzhou from an American prison. Meng was the chief financial officer of Huawei and the daughter of its founder.

Meng was arrested during the Trump administration in 2018 for bank and wire fraud. The government said she misled a financial institution to violate American sanctions on Iran.

But her culpability ran much deeper. The Huawei company has been the center of China's plan for global mind control.

Why did Biden let her go free?

China is a unique synthesis of an ideological communist state and an old-fashioned expansionist, imperialist police state. While China boasts a very impressive military with a large arsenal of nuclear weapons, it is the control of our minds, not our territory, that it covets.

The Chinese system of mind control currently holds its population—18 percent of the world's people, or 1.4 billion—under its sway and is based on repression, not conquest, and certainly not friendly persuasion.[1]

But to repress a billion and a half people is a bit of a task, and China has mobilized all its resources to do it. The government drills down to each individual man, woman, and child to monitor their every action, seeking to find signs of dissent or dissatisfaction. Then it uses its massive societal and economic power to isolate, quarantine, and punish dissenters.

Primary among the tools the Chinese government uses to suppress its people is a "social credit score" assigned to each person based on such public documents as criminal records, motor vehicle driving histories, and financial credit scores.

But it is also predicated on data that, in the West, is confidential and proprietary. Through its central bank digital currency (CBDC), the Chinese government monitors everything its citizens spend money on, from chewing gum to cars. If they use too much fossil fuel, patronize foreign websites, or give any indication of disloyalty, their scores plummet, meaning that they cannot get good jobs or apartments, their kids can't get into college, they cannot even use planes or trains.

OK, so China represses its own people. How does that affect us?

Because the government in Beijing wants to extend the social credit system worldwide.

It can do that without a single soldier or ship. It just needs to monitor the internet and assign each of us a social credit score, measured through their eyes.

If we flunk their ratings, China can use its power in the more than twenty-four hundred corporations in which it holds significant shares of stock to punish or marginalize us. For example, if you work for AMC, American Multi-Cinema, the largest movie theater company in the US, China can get to you. In 2012, Beijing-based Dalian Wanda Group became its majority stakeholder, giving them the power to make decisions at the executive level.

And let's say that China kept a social credit score on you and you flunked. How easy would it be for some mandarin in Beijing to hold up your promotion or get you fired? No questions asked . . . or answered.

If you work for any of the following companies, all of which China has acquired a significant financial and equity stake, it could be the same story:

- General Motors
- Spotify
- Snapchat
- Hilton Hotels and Resorts
- General Electric Appliance Division
- And many others

As China extends its influence around the globe, the number of Western corporations that can be forced to jump when requested gets longer and longer.

The key to the Chinese scheme is the social credit score. Huawei, the Chinese electronics firm that specializes in high-tech equipment, included in its 5G phones spyware that makes it possible to keep track of users and provide the material China can use to give each of us a social credit score.

The Trump administration clipped Huawei's wings when it cut off access to US technology, seeking to starve it of crucial components.

"We don't want their equipment in the United States because they spy on us," Trump told Fox News. "And any country that uses it, we're not going to do anything in terms of sharing intelligence."

The US Department of Commerce's new rules will further block Huawei from accessing chip technology.[2]

Washington cut off Huawei's access to US components and technology, including Google's music and other smartphone services, in August 2020.[3] Those penalties were raised last year when the White House barred vendors worldwide from using US technology to produce components for Huawei.

The move forced Huawei to become more of a conventional cell phone supplier and move away from 5G technology.

So when Trump had Huawei CFO Meng Wanzhou arrested in 2018, it was a big deal.

And Biden's decision to free her is inexplicable, except if we consider it part of the payback to the Beijing regime for its financial support of the corrupt Biden family.

This is just one of the questions we will focus on in the final chapters of this book: What did Biden get in return for all that Chinese money?

CHAPTER 28

BIDEN LETS CHINA OFF
THE GREEN HOOK

NOT TO BELABOR THE obvious, but we are one planet, and carbon emissions, whether from China, Europe, or the US, contribute equally to global climate change.

But Biden has repeatedly let Beijing off the hook for its uncurbed emission of carbon.

While the United States has cut its carbon emissions, China's have soared:

TABLE 28.1. PERCENT OF CO$_2$ EMISSIONS BY COUNTRY

	2000 (%)	2021 (%)
CHINA	14	31
US	24	14
EU	14	8
INDIA	7	4

Source: https://www.cnbc.com/2021/05/06/chinas-greenhouse-gas-emissions-exceed-us-developed-world-report.html.

In 2000, the US accounted for 24 percent of global carbon emissions, but by 2021, its share had dropped almost by half, to 14 percent. But China went in the opposite direction. In 2000, it emitted only 14 percent of the world's carbon, but in 2021, its share had more than doubled to 31 percent.

China argues that its immense size causes it, inevitably, to emit masses of carbon, but India's relatively low emissions levels belie that argument. With China and India basically tied for the lead in world population (in 2023, China had 1,439 billion and India had 1,380 billion), there is no good reason why China emits eight times as much carbon as India.

The Paris Climate Accords, signed in 2015, permit each country to establish its own goals for carbon emission reduction.

All the signatories but China stepped up with pledges to curb emissions both immediately and over the long term.

But China, pleading that it was an underdeveloped country, said that it would continue to increase its carbon emissions through 2030, at which point they would peak and then, we hope, drop to net zero by 2060.

China maintains that it needs the extra time to catch up to the rest of the industrialized world. As it does so, Beijing maintains China should be given the same opportunities to emit carbon as Europe and the US had as their economies grew in the last two centuries.

What a specious argument!

We are one planet, and pollution anywhere causes damage everywhere.

And then there is the example of India, whose GDP is rising by 8.4 percent a year, even as it cuts its carbon emissions in half!

The fact is that the Paris Accords and other measures to limit carbon emissions are slowing the growth of the US economy while doing nothing to slow China's. While we attenuate our production of goods and services to keep our carbon emissions low, China does not and acquires a tremendous quantitative advantage over the United States.

Seeing this disparity, Donald Trump, as president, pulled the US out of the Paris Accords because of its failure to rein in Chinese emissions. But Biden, during his first day in office, restored the US to the Paris Climate Accords, putting us back on the leash Trump had shaken off. (And the US continued to lead the world in carbon emission reductions, slicing our carbon output by more than the rest of the world combined.)

And China continues to increase its carbon emissions by leaps and bounds. In 2022, it increased its carbon emissions by 1.3 percent, triggered by a 3.3 percent rise in coal consumption.[1]

And again, the question nags, Was Biden seeking to appease his domestic political constituency by agreeing to the Paris Accords and letting China spew as much carbon into our atmosphere as they want, or was he repaying China for the massive funding it gave his family?

CHAPTER 29

BIDEN LETS CHINA CIRCLE THE GLOBE

CHINA HAS DESPERATELY SOUGHT to increase its foreign diplomatic and military presence throughout the world, overcoming centuries of isolation.

Its main vehicle, started by President Xi Jinping in 2013, is the Belt and Road Initiative. The name comes from the medieval Silk Road, built in the fourteenth and fifteenth centuries by the Mongols to connect Asia to Europe and traveled by famed explorer Marco Polo to go from his native Venice to China.

The modern Silk Road, proposed by Xi, is a vast global infrastructure development program funded by Chinese government investments and loans to more than 150 countries and international organizations. The transportation network was originally devised to link East Asia and Europe through physical infrastructure. But in the past decade, the goals of the road have become more ambitious and expanded to include Africa, Oceania, and Latin America.

China is helping countries build ports, skyscrapers, railroads, roads, bridges, airports, dams, coal-fired power stations, and tunnels.

The initiative has been compared to the post–World War II Marshall Plan, which helped Europe back to its feet after the devastation of the war.

But there are two crucial differences: the Marshall Plan gave money to Europe, and the Belt and Road Initiative makes loans that must be repaid with interest. The aid to Europe went to democracies, while the Belt and Road Initiative focuses on aid to autocratic governments.

The program amounts to what has been classically called a "debt trap" where countries borrow so much money that they, in effect, must end up surrendering their economic or political independence to their creditor: China.

The pattern in the Belt and Road Initiative has repeated itself countless times: a Chinese official visits a third-world country and meets with its dictator. "You need an airport," he might say, or maybe it's a renovation of a port or some other expensive capital project. You can almost see the foreign dictator drooling.

As a dictator, usually backed by military force, he can incur whatever debt he pleases and leave it for the people of his country to pay back, often long after he is gone.

The nation may not need an airport or a new port, but the dictator certainly welcomes the loan anyway, realizing that he can put it in his Swiss bank account with impunity. His people, who have no say in the process, would not have to pay the funds back for several years or even decades, and he can show off all the good he is doing in the meantime.

In the years since the Belt and Road Initiative started, China has lent over one trillion yuan ($160 billion) to third-world countries. The loans are typically negotiated in secret and need no approval from any representative body in the borrowing country. Yet it puts these largely poor countries on the hook for billions in loans.

In the 1960s and 1970s, David Rockefeller, CEO of Chase Manhattan Bank, went around the world lending huge sums to third-world countries. Seeing opportunities to sign up dictators and kings so he could charge high-interest rates, Chase became a global power.

US policymakers had to work overtime in the 1980s and 1990s to negotiate debt forgiveness schemes so the loan recipients could get out of hock and back on their feet.

But China also has an ulterior motive in the Belt and Road Initiative. It often lends to countries, particularly in Africa with vast natural resources—including rare earth minerals. China often uses these resources as collateral. When the borrower defaults, China inherits its mines and minerals, furthering its goal of global domination of the rare earth mineral market.

So China's generosity in extending Belt and Road Initiative loans is really a geopolitical gambit to share in the mineral wealth of Africa. The pattern is set: Lend a dictator money he doesn't need for a project the nation really doesn't want. Then wait for the dictator to pocket the money, hiding it in his Swiss bank account. When the loans fall into default, China gets to foreclose and seize the mining rights it negotiated to be the loan's collateral.

In 2011, China approved the merger of its three biggest rare earth mineral mining companies to create the China Rare Earth Group, which controlled one-third of its rare earth mineral production.

The new company used the Belt and Road Initiative to acquire mines in a range of countries. China tells the world that it is only trying to "assure the stability of production," but its efforts to corner the market on these minerals are transparent.

As Felix K. Chang writes for the Foreign Policy Research Institute, "For Beijing, assurance of 'the stability of production and supply chains' amounts to more than control over the physical production of rare earth metals; it also means the ability to influence their prices, much like the way the OPEC cartel tries to manage the price of oil. That ability is clearly a priority for China's Ministry of Industry and Information Technology (MIIT)."[1]

China already demonstrated its willingness to use its domination of the rare earth mineral industry for its imperial purposes. When Japan nationalized the Senkaku Islands, uninhabited islets off the coast of Japan, in 2009—territory China claimed as its own—Beijing embargoed exports of the minerals to Tokyo. Japan caved in to China's pressure in 2014 by acknowledging that "China has a case as well" and giving China an opening to argue that there is indeed a territorial dispute over the islands.[2]

Chang writes, "It turns out rare earth metals are not so rare; they are found all over the world."[3] Particularly in Africa. As noted by the Observer Research Foundation, "Currently, the global annual demand for rare earth elements (REEs) is largely met by China, which has devoted itself to increasing its presence in Africa guaranteeing ambitious energy and technological transitions."[4]

In all, the world mining production was 280,000 metric tons in 2021. China accounted for 168,000 of that output (60 percent). The US share was only 43,000 (15 percent).[5] In the year between 2020 and 2021, China expanded its mining output from 140,000 metric tons to 168,000—an increase of 20 percent. At the same time, the US mine production rose from 39,000 metric tons in 2020 to 43,000 in 2021, an increase of only 10 percent.

The foundation explains, "Chinese control over mine production works in two different ways. First, the Chinese companies downstream the processing of rare earth elements back in China, ensuring ownership control over the mining production. Second, as African markets are small with a limited fiscal base, they are forced to resort to international financing sources. Since the 2000s, China has been the single largest creditor in Africa and has played a key role in bilateral negotiations and strategies regarding finance. Given the transactional nature of foreign policy, China uses its economic leverage to achieve its long-term goals in the African continent."[6]

And when African countries try to elude China's influence and spurn loans from Beijing for infrastructure improvements they don't need, the US often punishes them for their boycott of China's Belt and Road Initiative.

Sierra Leone, a tiny democracy—one of the very few in West Africa—refused to borrow $400 million from China for a new airport and a host of infrastructure projects. Sierra Leone's president, Julius Maada Bio, knew that China's generosity was tied to his country's vast uranium deposits and canceled the agreement in October 2018.[7]

As China pressed its case and tried to inveigle the country of seven million people to borrow massively so it could acquire liens on its natural resources, one would have expected the US to back Sierra Leone's efforts to avoid Chinese domination and remain free of its financial tentacles. But quite the opposite happened: the US has recently been an outspoken critic of President Bio.[8]

Bio is one of a handful of West Africa's democratically elected leaders. In 2018, Julius Maada Bio was elected president of Sierra Leone with 51.8 percent of the vote.

After his first successful term, he was reelected, with over 55 percent of the vote—the threshold he needed to avoid a runoff. And while the US has done very little to condemn the many dictatorships in West Africa—all of whom have played ball with China—the Biden administration has attacked Bio and tried to declare his 2023 reelection illegitimate. It appears that there is a price Biden imposes for countries and leaders who say no to his Chinese sponsors.[9]

But popular resistance to the exploitation of resources by China has increased. Even in authoritarian states like Russia and Kazakhstan, the Belt and Road Initiative projects have been met with demonstrations and protests.

- A Chinese-financed water-bottling plant on Lake Baikal in Siberia was killed after a court decision—backed by popular protests—said that drawing water from the world's largest freshwater resource would hurt the environment.
- In Zhanaozen, an impoverished oil town in western Kazakhstan, rumors spread that China planned to relocate fifty-five factories to Kazakhstan along with their Chinese workers to run them. People protested the planned influx of Chinese workers.[10]
- As reported in *Fortune*, "In Pakistan, millions of textile workers have been laid off because the country has too much foreign debt and can't afford to keep the electricity on and machines running."[11]
- In Kenya, the government has held back paychecks to thousands of civil service workers to save cash to pay foreign loans. The president's chief economic adviser tweeted last month, "Salaries or default? Take your pick."[12]
- The Belt and Road Initiative loans proved so burdensome to Sri Lanka that it defaulted after ousting the government that agreed to the loans. Half a million industrial jobs have vanished, inflation has pierced 50 percent, and more than half the population in many parts of the country has fallen into poverty.[13]
- In Pakistan, demonstrators shut down Gwadar, Pakistan's port city, as they protested a massive Chinese development plan. The protests were so severe that a suicide bomber attacked Chinese motorists, killing two children. Militants accuse China of exploiting local mineral resources.

The *Guardian* reported, "Under the project, Pakistan surren-
dered Gwadar port to a Chinese-backed multinational corporation for a lease of 40 years." The Pakistan government accepted
China's investment in the hope it would help boost the country's
ailing economy. "But Balochistan is home to a long-running
violent insurgency, and China's presence in Gwadar has been
the cause of much social unrest and led to great anti-Chinese
sentiment."[14]

Fortune reported, "A dozen poor countries are facing economic instability and even collapse under the weight of hundreds of billions of dollars in foreign loans, much of them from
the world's biggest and most unforgiving government lender,
China."[15]

The Associated Press reports that Pakistan, Kenya, Zambia,
Laos, Mongolia, and many others are finding that their debt
repayments are cutting into the revenues they need to keep
schools open, provide electricity, and pay for food and fuel.[16]

China won't forgive the debt, and it now appears that China
insists that it come before any other creditor and requires bor-
rowers to put money into escrow.

And the debts to China are coming due. As Harvard economist Ken Rogoff said, "In a lot of the world, the clock has
hit midnight."[17]

CHAPTER 30

CHINA PUTS A MILITARY BASE IN CUBA, AND BIDEN LETS THEM DO IT

IN OCTOBER 1962, PRESIDENT John F. Kennedy almost plunged the world into a nuclear war when Cuban dictator Fidel Castro agreed to let Russia put missile bases on his island. War was only narrowly averted when the Russian ships carrying the missiles turned around.

On June 8, 2023, the *Wall Street Journal* reported that China and Cuba were "at an advanced stage" in negotiations to "establish a new joint military training facility on the island [that] could lead to the stationing of Chinese troops just 100 miles off Florida's coast."[1] Two days after the *Wall Street Journal* story, the White House "confirmed publicly that Chinese intelligence collection facilities are, indeed, already in Cuba."

What Kennedy almost started a world war to prevent, China is now doing right under our noses with apparent impunity.

The Cuban bases would be part of a wider network of over a hundred commercial ports and terminals in which China has invested recently. A US Pentagon report says that these bases could be "dual use," allowing China to "interfere with US military operations and to support offensive operations against the United States."[2]

CHAPTER 31

CHINA USES BELT AND ROAD INITIATIVE TO BUILD MILITARY BASES

THE CHINESE BELT AND Road Initiative not only seeks to give China access to strategic mineral resources in the third world but also looks to pave the way for Chinese military bases around the globe.[1]

China built its first overseas base in 2017 in Djibouti, Africa. Djibouti, a tiny country with a population of about one million, is strategically located in the Horn of Africa, just across the Gulf of Aden from Yemen. Its location has led both China and the US to establish military bases there.

China, in 2023, is currently racing to complete its second overseas base, the Ream Naval Base, in Cambodia, which is expected to be completed soon.

The *Washington Post* published classified documents from China in 2023 suggesting that it plans three more bases in addition to the one in Djibouti and the one under construction in Cambodia. One of the new bases would be in the United Arab Emirates, right on the Persian Gulf; one in Tanzania; and one in Gabon.[2]

Beyond conventional military bases, US intelligence is following what Beijing calls Project 141, which is aimed at giving the People's Liberation Army military bases and logistics platforms abroad by 2030, possibly in Mozambique, Equatorial Guinea, Tanzania, and Tajikistan in Central Asia.[3]

Biden's response to this economic and military threat has been pathetic. He announced a worldwide version of the Build Back Better Plan he advertised in his presidential campaign to counter China's Belt and Road Initiative.[4] But it faltered after his allies refused to kick in. Biden rebranded his program the Partnership for Global Infrastructure and Investment, pledging $600 billion over five years, largely from private investors.[5]

The US would contribute $200 billion in total, though it's unclear what the split would be between private and public sector funding and how the government plans to convince companies to take part.

As China races ahead to corner the world's rare earth mineral mines, the United States, under Biden, lags with no definite program of its own to secure mines in Africa and is hobbled by a president who refuses to allow rare earth mineral mining because he says it conflicts with his environmental agenda. It seems not to have occurred to the addled president that without the minerals that come from these mines, he will have no electric cars, solar panels, or wind turbines to power his green dreams.

We return again to our troubling question, Does Biden's refusal to expand vigorously our rare earth mineral program stem from disorganization or a lack of clarity in setting priorities, or does it signal a willingness to concede this vital natural resource to China because his family is beholden to them for the money they have made?

CHAPTER 32

CHINA'S MILITARY CHALLENGE

WHILE CHINA SEEKS TO undermine US security and freedom's capacity to survive through mind-control strategies, its more conventional military challenge also bears scrutiny.

The Pentagon describes China as posing a "pacing challenge" to American military might. This odd choice of words makes it sound as if the two countries were runners in a track-and-field competition as opposed to deadly adversaries in a potential global war.

But the fact is that China's military budget has continued to grow at roughly a 7 percent annual rate. China now spends an estimated $250 billion to $300 billion a year on its armed forces—1.6 percent of its GDP—second worldwide only to America's 3.5 percent.[1]

China is now in the midst of the largest military buildup since World War II. Geopolitical Intelligence Services (GIS) reports, "In the seven years between 2015 and 2021, Beijing spent as much on its military as it did during the 21 years before 2015."[2]

And China is using its military power. While it has not waged a shooting war since 1979, it is menacing peace throughout Asia and the Pacific.

China increasingly threatens to invade Taiwan, the breakaway province that left the mainland as Mao overthrew the nationalist regime of Chiang Kai-Shek in 1949. Beijing regards Taiwan as still part of China and makes no secret of its plans to seize control of the island—by force, if necessary.

For a while, China tried to lure Taiwan to cede its independence by holding out the prospect of regional autonomy and self-government. But when China broke similar promises to Hong Kong after it took over, Taiwan became justifiably suspicious of Chinese intentions.

China also menaces free shipping in the East China and the South China Seas, asserting increasing Chinese sovereignty over both waterways: "Since 2009, China has claimed most of the South China Sea as its own, an assertion dismissed by its neighbors Brunei, Indonesia, Malaysia, the Philippines, Taiwan and Vietnam. Recently, two ships from the China Coast Guard almost struck one from the Philippines Coast Guard."[3]

China claims the Senkaku Islands for itself and recently defied Japan by sending four China Coast Guard vessels around the islands for eighty hours, disobeying Japanese orders to leave.

Finally, China has built and militarized at least seven artificial islands in the South China Sea, creating more than twenty-four hundred acres of new land since 2013, heightening fears in Vietnam and the Philippines, which also have interests there.

At home, China has about four hundred nuclear warheads, and the Pentagon fears it will expand its arsenal to between one thousand and fifteen hundred by 2035. While the US has five thousand warheads, China's growing capacity is not good news.

But it is China's naval buildup that worries the US the most. China boasts the largest navy in the world, with 340 warships to the United States' 300. The US Navy hit a low of 270 ships in 2016, but Trump built it up to 300 by the end of his term, still 30 fewer than China has. And Beijing expects to grow its fleet to 400 ships in the next two years.

The Pentagon counters that its ships are much larger than China's and its total tonnage is 4.5 million, as opposed to Beijing's less than two million.

While China builds up its navy, the ever-compliant China stooge Joe Biden proposes cuts to the US Navy that the *Washington Free Beacon* reports "would force it to prematurely retire almost a dozen ships and take offline critical missile systems that serve as a primary deterrent to Chinese aggression."[4]

"By taking these ships out of action," the *Washington Free Beacon* explains, "the Navy would lose more than 600 vertical launch missile systems—a missile capability that serves as the primary deterrent to Chinese military attacks in the Pacific."[5]

Biden disregarded repeated requests from the Marine Corps for a minimum of thirty-one amphibious warships, which would serve a critical role in any military conflict with China. Three of these ships are being retired, and the Biden administration is expected to order a "strategic pause" in the purchase of modernized warships, leaving the force below its statutory requirement of thirty-one ships.

Perhaps the greatest drain on our military resources, as we face a possible Chinese invasion of Taiwan, is the expenditure of ammunition, missiles, and shells by Ukraine in its war with Russia. In his haste to help Ukraine repel the Russian invasion, Biden has depleted our arsenal of weapons. What better favor could he do China as it eyes an invasion of Taiwan?

The *Wall Street Journal* reports, "The war in Ukraine has depleted American stocks of some types of ammunition and the Pentagon has been slow to replenish its arsenal, sparking concerns among US officials that American military readiness could be jeopardized by the shortage."[6]

The United States has supplied Ukraine with sixteen rocket launchers, known as HIMARS, and thousands of guns, drones, missiles, and other equipment. Much of that, including ammunition, has come directly from US inventory, depleting stockpiles intended for unexpected threats.

The *Wall Street Journal* reported, "One of the most lethal weapons the Pentagon has sent to Ukraine are howitzers that fire high-explosive 155mm ammunition weighing about 100 pounds each and able to accurately hit targets dozens of miles away. But, in recent weeks, the *Journal* said that the inventory of 155mm combat rounds in U.S. military storage have become 'uncomfortably low.' The levels aren't yet critical because the U.S. isn't engaged in any major military conflict, but, as one defense official said, 'It is not at the level we would like to go into combat.'"[7]

Defense analysts blame Biden for the shortfall in ammo. "This was knowable. It was foreseeable. It was forewarned, including from industry leaders to the Pentagon. And it was easily fixable," said Mackenzie Eaglen, a senior fellow at the American Enterprise Institute, a think tank in Washington.[8]

"What is needed," she said, "is for the government to spend money to fix the problem."[9]

But perhaps Biden did not anticipate the problem his drawdown of ammunition would create. The *Wall Street Journal* reported, "In the U.S., it takes 13 to 18 months from the time orders are placed for munitions to be manufactured," according to an industry official. "Replenishing stockpiles of more sophisticated weaponry such as missiles and drones can take much longer. Even a yearlong delay is a problem precisely because ammunition shortages can pop up quickly given the rate they can be drawn down in a conflict."[10]

Speaking on an earnings call on July 19, 2022, Jim Taiclet, chief executive of Lockheed Martin Corporation, said the Pentagon has yet to put the contracts in place or coordinate with the industry to buy more supplies, a process that often takes two to three years.[11]

The Defense Department needs to "shift gears" if it wants the industry to prepare for more orders, he said. "And I can tell you the clutch isn't engaged yet."[12]

But, of course, the president needs to lead the way, and there is no evidence that Biden has done so. Indeed, his proposed cuts in the defense budget point in the other direction.

In fact, Biden delivered $83 billion in advanced military equipment to the Taliban after he abandoned Afghanistan. Much of the weaponry has ended up in Chinese hands.[13]

China is probably closely studying US military readiness as it decides whether to invade Taiwan. This is no time to be caught with empty guns. Biden should, obviously, have realized that if he is sending supplies to Ukraine, they must be replenished. But Biden likely did not want to be provocative toward China, especially after all it had done for him and his family!

Or has Biden deliberately scrapped the bottom of our barrel of military equipment to give it to the other great benefactor of the Biden crime family—Ukraine?

When Russia invaded Ukraine, the blatant imperialism and aggression generated massive sympathy for the embattled, wronged, smaller nation.

But as the war has gone on and the initial Russian thrust was effectively blunted, the war has come down to a battle for control of the Donbas region, only 15 percent of Ukraine's territory. In a World War I–style slugfest, vast casualties on both sides have been recorded, and millions have been forced to leave their homes and become refugees.

The war, as noted, has drained US military stockpiles and cost us $75 billion in foreign aid. And there is no end in sight.

This level of human and financial cost begs the question, Is Donbas worth it?

But we cannot ignore the millions paid by Ukrainian sources to the Biden family in alleged bribes. Has this money played a role in the president's willingness to denude our own military preparedness to fund a war over two provinces in Ukraine?[14]

CHAPTER 33

CHINA'S NEW WEAPONS

Paid for by the US Trade Deficit

WHILE BIDEN HAS DEPLETED our weapon stockpiles to fight the war in Ukraine, China has been using its half-a-trillion-dollar trade surplus with the US to arm itself to the teeth.

These weapons are not for some hypothetical future war but, in many cases, to be used in a planned and likely forthcoming invasion of Taiwan.

China is "on the verge of fielding some of the most modern weapon systems in the world," says a new US defense intelligence assessment.[1]

Here are the seven weapons systems China is developing that US defense analysts fear the most:[2]

1. THE ELECTROMAGNETIC RAIL GUN

Chinese state media says that Chinese warships will "soon" be equipped with naval rail guns capable of hitting targets at great distances. China's *Global Times* reported, "China's naval electromagnetic weapon and equipment have surpassed other countries and become a world leader."[3]

China has suggested that the technology could be used to develop electromagnetic catapults for China's future aircraft carriers.

2. CHINA'S VERSION OF THE "MOTHER OF ALL BOMBS"

The China North Industries Group Corporation Limited, a major Chinese defense-industry corporation, has, according to Chinese media, developed a massive conventional weapon for China's bombers known as the "Chinese version of the 'Mother of All Bombs'"—China's largest nonnuclear bomb.

The *New York Post* reports that although China is using the same nickname as the US uses for its superbomb—MOAB (Mother of All Bombs)—"the Chinese weapon is smaller and lighter than its American counterpart. The weapon would likely be carried by the Chinese Xi'an H-6K bombers. The American version is so large that it has to be carried by a C-130."[4]

3. "CARRIER-KILLER" MISSILES

The *New York Post* reports, "The DF-26 ballistic missile is not a new weapon, but China recently released, for the first time, video footage of an exercise involving the weapon, which is reportedly able to carry conventional and nuclear warheads for strikes against land and sea targets. The DF-26 is commonly referred to as a 'carrier killer.' The video revealed certain features suggesting the missile is a capable anti-ship weapon with the ability to take out a US aircraft carrier."[5] Analysts speculate that China is drawing attention to the missile's capability to be sure the US realizes its potential risk to US carriers and bases.

4. GUNS THAT SHOOT AROUND CORNERS

Chinese state media said last month that the Chinese military is arming its special forces with "sci-fi" weapons—"futuristic individual combat weapons like grenade-launching assault rifles, corner shot pistols and knife guns."[6]

Citing a Beijing military expert, the *Global Times* said China was developing "supersoldiers" who would be able to take on ten enemy combatants at one time. The Chinese military is undergoing a massive overhaul with the goal of creating a world-class fighting force.[7]

5. THE STEALTH DRONE "SKY HAWK"

CCTV recently aired a video showcasing China's stealth drone "Sky Hawk" taking flight for the first time.[8]

Experts suggested that the unmanned aircraft could be launched from China's future aircraft carriers.

Chinese military experts said the US maintains an edge in this area, having developed the Northrop Grumman X-47B carrier-based drone, but both China and Russia are rushing to develop stealth drones for future missions.

6. UPGRADED STEALTH FIGHTER

The *New York Post* reports, "China is considering the development of a twin-seat variant of the J-20 stealth fighter, which would be a first for fifth-generation aircraft. . . . Chinese media said the aircraft would be capable of tactical bombing missions or electronic warfare, not just air superiority."[9]

It added that having aircraft variations "other countries do not possess will greatly expand the Chinese military's capability in an asymmetric warfare," the *Global Times* said, citing Chinese analysts.[10]

7. UNDERGROUND BUNKERS AND INTERCONTINENTAL BALLISTIC MISSILE STRIKE

Apart from its focus on conventional and theater weapons, Chinese troops have reportedly been conducting simulated intercontinental ballistic missile (ICBM) exercises from underground bunkers, the *Business Insider* reports.[11]

The nuclear-attack exercises, which are aimed at simulated enemies, are designed to improve China's counterattack (second-strike) capability in the event a war breaks out, Chinese media explained. The strategic bunkers where the drills were staged are referred to as China's "underground Great Wall" by Qian Qihu, the man who designed them.

He said the drill was "about signaling China's modernizing nuclear deterrence. It is about telling the Americans and others that China has a credible second-strike capability and that it is determined to use it if it comes under nuclear attack and it is, in part a message from Beijing to the US about the ultimate perils of escalation."[12]

Significantly, China put all these new and modernized weapons on public display at an arms show in 2019, saving US intelligence the task of ferreting out the information. Their motive can only have been to warn the US of Chinese capabilities should they attack Taiwan.

	US	China

CHAPTER 34

CHINA'S SPACE RACE

THE COMPARISONS WE HAVE just reviewed between the United
States' and China's naval capabilities and resources have a
haunting relevance today as China contemplates an invasion of
Taiwan. But any future analysis of the relative power of the two
nations must begin with their ability to project technology and
power in space.

China only started its space program with its first satellite
launch in 1970, but it has moved swiftly to try to catch up to
the United States.

The stats indicate a decisive and significant American advantage, still, in space:

TABLE 34.1. US LEADS SPACE RACE—BUT CHINA IS CATCHING-UP![1]

	US	China
SPENDING	$30 billion	$8.9 billion
ACTIVE SATELLITES	3,433	541
ACTIVE SPACEPORTS	7	4
PLANNED SPACEPORTS	13	2

Source: https://theconversation.com/is-the-us-in-a-space-race-against-china-203473.

Writing in the journal *Conversation*, Svetla Ben-Itzhak, professor of space and international relations at Air University, rejects the notion of a "space race" between Washington and Beijing but instead describes their rivalry as a "complex hegemony," where the US is still dominating in key space capabilities, and this lead is further amplified by a strong network of partners.

The US space program also differs from China's in that it has several nonmilitary academic and commercial applications. Sixty-one percent of our rocket launches were for nonmilitary purposes, such as Earth observation or telecommunications, while 84 percent of China's were for government or military payloads intended mostly for electronic intelligence and optical imaging.

Despite this lead, the Pentagon published a report in August 2022 predicting that China would surpass US space capabilities as early as 2045.

Both countries want to land on the moon, but China is working mainly with Russia, while the US has joined with twenty-four countries in the Artemis Accords with the aim to return mankind to the moon by 2025 and establish a moon base and lunar space station shortly thereafter.

Ben-Itzhak writes, "In addition to the broad international participation, the Artemis Program has contracted with a staggering number of private companies to develop a range of technologies, from lunar landers to lunar construction methods and more."[2]

But Ralph Jennings, writing for Voice of America, points out, "China now has the technology, hardware and know-how to coordinate a war from space. . . . The People's Liberation Army could park military equipment systems in space or use satellites to surveil the ground and may eventually use sensors to detect enemy submarines at sea."[3]

Military analysts suggest that "the Chinese military would most likely use military technology in space to seek control in the disputed East and South China seas and fend off challenges on the high seas of the Western Pacific just beyond China's near seas."[4]

China demonstrated how it could use and militarize space in 2006 when it conducted a military experiment and destroyed one of its own weather satellites while it was orbiting around the Earth. Since most American defense systems these days rely on satellites or GPS technology (just like in your car!), any war is sure to start with attempts to shoot down the opponent's satellites, and China's test showed how aggressively it would use space if conflict broke out.

The debris from the Chinese shoot-down has cluttered up space ever since. Satellites, astronauts, space stations, and missiles alike now must dodge fragments of the satellite as they orbit peacefully around the globe. The debris is not likely to crash to Earth for years. Experts say the destroyed satellite contributed more debris to space than all other human interventions combined over the past fifty years. In all, more than six hundred shrapnel objects have been detected, and another three hundred are expected to be found in the years—and decades—to come.

But China will not get so much as a citation or a ticket for littering.

CHAPTER 35

THE UNKEPT PROMISE

How China Is Breaking Its Commitment to Free World Trade

WHEN BILL CLINTON ACCEDED to China's inclusion in the WTO, the world heralded it as a great moment for global civilization.

The *Economist* wrote that it hoped that "economic integration would encourage China to evolve into a market economy and that, as they grew wealthier, its people would come to yearn for democratic freedoms, rights and the rule of law."[1]

WTO director general Dr. Supachai Panitchpakdi gushed, "It is virtually impossible to overstate the importance of bringing the world's most populous nation into a system that establishes internationally accepted rules for economic behavior. The WTO will set out the rules for a market-based economy. . . . The agreement signals China's willingness to play by international trade rules and to bring its often opaque and cumbersome governmental apparatus into harmony with a world order that demands clarity and fairness."[2]

That was then, and this is now. The *Economist* now sings a different tune: "The illusion has been shattered" that China will integrate into the liberal international order.[3]

At first, China showed some interest in market opening after its accession to the WTO, but when Xi Jinping came to power in 2013, the candle of reform was extinguished, along with some of its advocates.

Indeed, China saw WTO membership as protection against having to reform, giving it carte blanche to ignore trade enforcement measures other member nations might take.

China's flouting of the WTO rules was so egregious that the Trump administration launched an investigation into China's trade and economic practices. The effort culminated in the imposition of tariffs on approximately $350 billion worth of Chinese exports to the United States—that's about 66 percent of Chinese exports to America at an average tariff rate of 19 percent.

The Information Technology and Innovation Foundation (ITIF) ranked sixty countries on its 2019 Global Mercantilist Index. Mercantilism is the global economic system that preceded capitalism and stressed the national acquisition of gold rather than the development of industry and trade as the way to create wealth.

The Global Mercantilist Index measures how much countries adopt "beggar-thy-neighbor" economic strategies that try to hoard resources rather than use them to generate trade. It based its ratings on eighteen variables, such as "market access restrictions, forced localization of production, currency manipulation, IP theft, digital protectionism, and benefits for domestically owned enterprises, among others."[4] The report found that China is in a class of its own when it comes to mercantilism—it was the only country to score in the "high" category.

China encodes its mercantile trade policies in its Company Law, which requires that all private or state-owned enterprises (SOEs) have a CCP organization that "management must listen to."[5]

The ITIF recommends that the US revoke China's permanent MFN trading status and go back to the law that predated the 2002 grant of "permanent normal trade relations" to China.

Back then, China's MFN status had to be renewed annually by the US Congress. ITIF writes, "Because annual congressional debates on MFN renewal led to sustained pressure on China on issues such as human rights and unfair trade practices,"[6] it recommends returning to the conditional grant of approval that must be renewed annually.

The ITIF says that the "United States could return to the practice of annually applying MFN 'conditionally,' with a link to labor rights and environmental protections. Furthermore, if China consistently refuses to adhere to MFN commitments, the United States and its allies should consider renegotiating market access levels for goods and services at the WTO."[7]

But under Biden, it's not happening.

CORRUPT

CHAPTER 36

HERE'S WHAT CHINA GOT FROM THE BIDENS

SO LET'S SUM UP what China got from the Bidens:

- China received no international investigation into the source of the COVID-19 virus and no international sanctions for allowing it to leak from its lab in Wuhan, China.
- Biden ended American energy independence by canceling the Keystone Pipeline, killing permits for drilling offshore and on federal land, and letting the price of energy skyrocket without any effort to develop domestic sources.[1]
- Hunter's "investments" through the government-controlled Bank of China helped Beijing develop advanced facial recognition software to identify dissidents.
- Biden's Justice Department released Meng Wanzhou, daughter of the founder of Huawei.

- Through the development of 5G, Huawei and other companies have planted spyware in hundreds of millions of personal computers worldwide, allowing it to enforce its "personal responsibility score" to make people go along with China's policies.
- Biden agreed not to require China to commit to any carbon reduction goals in the Paris Accords until 2030.
- Promoting the green agenda, electric cars, solar batteries, and wind turbines, which need rare earth minerals from China to operate, Biden has replaced our dependence on Arab sheiks with a subservience to Chinese communists.
- Biden has killed plans for the largest US rare earth mineral mine in Minnesota.
- Biden let China launch the Belt and Road Initiative in 150 countries—without any effective US response—to give it access to rare earth minerals in dozens of foreign countries.
- Biden let China use the Belt and Road Initiative to open its second overseas military base with plans for four more, including a military base in Cuba, fewer than one hundred miles from the US.
- Biden stood by as China trapped dozens of nations into perpetual debt to China to pay for Belt and Road Initiative projects.
- Biden opened the door for US companies to move to China and give it their trade secrets and technology, giving it a global competitive edge.

- Biden worked with big retailers in the US to eviscerate the patent and copyright protection of intellectual property.
- By uncontrolled deficit spending, Biden paved the way for the assault on the dollar's status as the global currency, encouraging BRICS countries to elbow the dollar aside.
- Biden weakened the US militarily by shipping much of our weapons stockpile to Ukraine with no plans to replace it soon.
- Biden allowed 350,000 Chinese students to study in the US, offering unparalleled opportunities for corporate espionage.
- Biden disbanded the FBI's China Initiative to fight Chinese espionage.
- Biden allowed Saudi Arabia to become more and more of an ally to China.
- Biden did not object or sanction China when it manufactured 90 percent of the world's fentanyl, much of it to be shipped to our hemisphere and slipped in over our southern border.
- Biden cut back the US Navy's shipbuilding program so that it has now fallen further behind China.
- Though under the Clinton administration, Biden was a big supporter of the US granting China membership in the World Trade Organization and MFN trade status.

Conclusion

WAKE UP, AMERICA!

HOW IRONIC THAT AS the "woke" movement is sweeping America, we should have to really wake up our own country to the dangers it faces abroad.

It is obvious that China poses a mortal threat to the United States—the danger is so great, it bears repeating:

- China has a monopoly on rare earth minerals, which holds our environmental goals hostage.
- With Hunter Biden's assistance, China has developed a means of global mind control and planted it in computers all around us.
- China's spies are everywhere, getting our trade secrets illegally while our own companies give them away legally by moving to China and selling our country out in the process.

- China's agents have massively infiltrated our colleges and universities and profited handsomely from grants from our very own government.
- Through some distorted logic, we cripple our own industries and businesses to make them follow environmental regulations from which we exempt China.
- And as if all this were not enough to wake us up, China is challenging our domination of space, our naval supremacy, and our entire national defense program.

But China is not the real problem, not the real threat to our freedom. The corruption of our own elected leaders is the crux of our difficulties. Our laws do not prevent them from using their families to take bribes and payoffs before, during, and after they serve us in public office.

Stronger ethics laws embracing all the opportunities for theft that a big family offers are a partial answer. But the real answer is to stop electing weak people who succumb to Chinese entreaties to office.

It is too late to stop the godfather of the corrupt Biden family from entering the White House, but it's not too late to throw him out at the end of his first—and we hope only—term as president.

We have seen, throughout this book, how Donald J. Trump, when he was president, put the interests of our country first, often in the precise areas where Biden failed to do so.

- Trump avoided the inflation that invites our enemies to replace our currency at the peak of the global economy.

- Trump worked to expand our stocks of rare earth minerals and to repeal regulations that hamstring our production of these minerals.
- Trump withdrew from the Paris Climate Accords when he saw that it arbitrarily exempted China from compliance.
- Trump worked to stop Huawei and other Chinese companies from implanting spyware into our computers and even imprisoned a top Huawei official until Biden freed her.
- Trump demanded that China stop manipulating its currency, subsidizing its exports, and using its market to lure companies to steal their technology. Trump, realizing that all this conduct violated China's treaty obligations under the World Trade Organization, imposed tariffs to enforce the agreement.
- From the start of the COVID-19 pandemic, Trump laid the blame on China's doorstep and restricted travel by Chinese to the US within a month of the disease's appearance on our shores. Now he wants an international investigation to determine China's culpability in the pandemic. And if China refuses to cooperate, he proposes global sanctions to force it to do so.

There is no room for corruption at the top of our government and no excuse for not electing Donald J. Trump in 2024 to clean it up.

Notes

Preface

1 Peter Navarro and Greg Autry, *Death by China: Confronting the Dragon—a Global Call to Action*, 1st ed. (Pearson FT Press, 2011), 212.

2 https://www.cnn.com/ALLPOLITICS/1997/07/31/thompson/hearings.main/.

3 https://www.govinfo.gov/content/pkg/CRPT-105srpt167/pdf/CRPT-105srpt167-pt1.pdf.

4 https://www.csmonitor.com/Commentary/Opinion/2011/0921/Time-for-Obama-to-rethink-Washington-s-mild-mannered-stance-toward-China.

5 https://archive.nytimes.com/www.nytimes.com/library/world/asia/030900clinton-china-text.html.

6 Ibid.

7 Navarro and Autry, *Death by China*, 80.

8 Ibid., 80.

9 Ibid., 80.

Chapter 1: Up from Poverty

1 https://www.cbsnews.com/news/237-millionaires-in-congress/.
2 https://money.com/barack-obama-joe-biden-pension.
3 https://www.gobankingrates.com/net-worth/politicians/joe
-biden-net-worth/#:~:text=the%20past%20decade.-,Joe%20Biden
%27s%20Net%20Worth,worth%20at%20%249%20million%2C
%20however.
4 S corporations are small business corporations that are treated for
federal tax purposes as a partnership.
5 https://www.whitehouse.gov/disclosures/financial-disclosures/.

Chapter 2: The Missing $10 Million

1 https://money.com/barack-obama-joe-biden-pension/.
2 https://nypost.com/2022/04/09/hunter-biden-frequently-covered
-family-expenses-texts-reveal/.
3 Ibid.
4 https://www.breitbart.com/politics/2023/05/10/oversight-committee
-biden-family-business-received-over-10-million-from-romania
-china-for-unknown-work/.
5 https://www.breitbart.com/politics/2023/05/10/james-comer-names
-9-biden-family-members-business-payments/.
6 https://www.breitbart.com/politics/2023/06/17/james-comer
-predicts-biden-bank-records-show-family-accepted-up-30m-foreign
-business/.
7 https://oversight.house.gov/release/comer-releases-third-bank-memo
-detailing-payments-to-the-bidens-from-russia-kazakhstan-and
-ukraine%EF%BF%BC/.
8 Ibid.
9 https://www.breitbart.com/politics/2023/07/28/james-comer-raises
-concerns-of-biden-racketeering/.
10 https://www.breitbart.com/politics/2022/11/20/exclusive-comer
-bank-records-first-focus-biden-probe/.
11 https://www.finance.senate.gov/imo/media/doc/HSGAC%20
-%20Finance%20Joint%20Report%202020.09.23.pdf.

12 https://www.breitbart.com/politics/2023/07/17/james-comer-bidens
-owned-20-shell-companies-hide-payments-launder-money/.
13 Ibid.
14 https://oversight.house.gov/release/comer-reveals-new
-evidence-in-biden-familys-influence-peddling-schemes%EF
%BF%BC/.
15 Ibid.
16 Ibid.
17 Ibid.
18 Ibid.
19 Ibid.
20 https://oversight.house.gov/wp-content/uploads/2023/05/Bank
-Memorandum-5.10.23.pdf.
21 https://www.wsj.com/articles/devon-archer-joined-calls-joe-biden
-son-hunter-biden-264e66f0.
22 Ibid.
23 Ibid.
24 Ibid.
25 Ibid.
26 Ibid.
27 https://www.foxnews.com/category/person/joe-biden.
28 https://www.foxnews.com/politics/whistleblower-x-reveals-identity
-irs-special-agent-joseph-ziegler.
29 https://nypost.com/2023/07/19/foreign-nationals-gave
-biden-family-and-associates-over-17m-irs-whistleblower
-claims/.

Chapter 3: Mr. Biden Goes to Beijing

1 Peter Schweizer, *Profiles in Corruption: Abuse of Power by America's Progressive Elite* (Harper, 2020), 55.
2 Peter Schweizer, *Red-Handed: How American Elites Get Rich Helping China Win* (Harper, 2022), 10.
3 https://www.foxnews.com/politics/doj-fbi-irs-interfered-hunter
-biden-probe-according-whistleblower-testimony.

4   Schweizer, *Red-Handed*, 27.
5   https://freebeacon.com/biden-administration/16-bombshells-on
    -hunter-biden-from-the-irs-whistleblowers/.
6   Ibid.
7   Ibid.
8   Ibid.
9   Ibid.
10 Ibid.
11 Ibid.
12 Ibid.
13 https://global.upenn.edu/penn-biden-center/our-mission-statement.
14 https://www.forbes.com/sites/michelatindera/2020/10/22/how-the
    -bidens-earned-167-million-after-leaving-the-white-house/?sh=
    6bdca54e1e42.
15 https://oversight.house.gov/release/comer-anonymous-chinese
    -donations-to-upenn-potentially-influenced-biden-administration
    -policies%EF%BF%BC/.
16 Ibid.
17 https://freebeacon.com/campus/it-was-extraordinary-government
    -officials-were-stunned-by-startling-spike-in-chinese-donations-to
    -upenn-after-biden-think-tank-opened/.
18 https://newsdirect.com/news/tony-blinken-must-explain-anonymous
    -china-donations-to-penn-biden-center-which-he-managed
    -325774537.
19 Ibid.

Chapter 4: Mr. Biden Goes to Ukraine

1   https://www.hsgac.senate.gov/wp-content/uploads/imo/media/doc/
    HSGAC_Finance_Report_FINAL.pdf.
2   https://en.wikipedia.org/wiki/Vitaly_Yarema.
3   See https://www.hsgac.senate.gov/wp-content/uploads/imo/media/
    doc/HSGAC_Finance_Report_FINAL.pdf, https://www.grassley
    .senate.gov/news/news-releases/grassley-obtains-and-releases-fbi
    -record-alleging-vp-biden-foreign-bribery-scheme, and https://

nypost.com/2023/07/20/biden-bribe-file-released-burisma-chief-said
-both-joe-and-hunter-involved/.

4   https://nypost.com/2023/04/11/ex-biden-stenographer-says-fbi
-ignored-prezs-role-in-hunters-business-dealings/.

5   https://oversight.house.gov/release/comer-statement-on-fbis-refusal
-to-comply-with-congressional-subpoena%EF%BF%BC/#:~:text
=%E2%80%9CToday%2C%20the%20FBI%20informed%20the
,people%20is%20obstructionist%20and%20unacceptable.

6   https://obamawhitehouse.archives.gov/the-press-office/2014/04/21/
background-press-briefing-vice-president-bidens-trip-ukraine.

7   https://congress.gov/113/plaws/publ272/PLAW-113publ272.pdf.

8   https://thehill.com/people/chuck-grassley/.

9   https://thehill.com/people/viktor-shokin/.

10 https://thehill.com/homenews/house/4108735-republicans-release
-fbi-form-alleging-unverified-biden-burisma-allegations/.

11 https://nypost.com/2023/07/20/biden-bribe-file-released-burisma
-chief-said-both-joe-and-hunter-involved/#:~:text=Mykola
%20Zlochevsky%2C%20the%20owner%20of,the%20redacted
%20FD%2D1023%20form.

12 Ibid.

13 Ibid.

14 https://oversight.house.gov/release/comer-the-bidens-have-put
-themselves-first-and-america-last%EF%BF%BC/.

15 https://www.bbc.com/news/world-us-canada-66272217.

16 https://thehill.com/opinion/campaign/463307-solomon-these-once
-secret-memos-cast-doubt-on-joe-bidens-ukraine-story/.

17 Ibid.

18 https://www.nationalreview.com/2023/07/the-biden-familys
-history-of-influence-peddling-explained/; https://nypost.com/2021/
05/26/hunter-bidens-ukraine-salary-was-cut-after-joe-biden-left
-office/.

19 https://thehill.com/opinion/campaign/463307-solomon-these-once
-secret-memos-cast-doubt-on-joe-bidens-ukraine-story/.

20 Ibid.

Notes

21 https://www.hsgac.senate.gov/wp-content/uploads/imo/media/doc/HSGAC_Finance_Report_FINAL.pdf.

22 https://nypost.com/2023/05/25/comer-says-alleged-biden-bribe-was-5m-threatens-fbi-with-contempt-vote/?utm_campaign=iphone_nyp&utm_source=mail_app.

23 Ibid.

24 https://www.thegatewaypundit.com/2023/08/explosive-video-ukrainian-prosecutor-viktor-shokin-responds-bidens/?utm_source=rss&utm_medium=rss&utm_campaign=explosive-video-ukrainian-prosecutor-viktor-shokin-responds-bidens.

25 Ibid.

26 Ibid.

27 https://greeknewsondemand.com/2023/08/05/explosive-video-former-ukrainian-prosecutor-viktor-shokin-responds-to-bidens-corruption-accusations-and-reveals-shocking-details-about-his-dismissal-and-burisma-investigation/?utm_source=rss&utm_medium=rss&utm_campaign=explosive-video-former-ukrainian-prosecutor-viktor-shokin-responds-to-bidens-corruption-accusations-and-reveals-shocking-details-about-his-dismissal-and-burisma-investigation.

28 https://www.hsgac.senate.gov/wp-content/uploads/imo/media/doc/HSGAC_Finance_Report_FINAL.pdf.

29 Schweizer, *Profiles in Corruption*, 75.

30 https://nypost.com/2023/03/02/unsanctioned-russians-shopped-us-land-with-hunter-biden-dined-with-joe/.

31 https://www.forbes.com/profile/vladimir-yevtushenkov/?sh=667121301dce.

32 Ibid.

33 https://www.eureporter.co/world/russia/2022/03/23/russian-oligarch-who-makes-drone-bombers-to-destroy-ukraine-still-not-sanctioned/.

34 Ibid.

35 https://en.wikipedia.org/wiki/Kronshtadt_Orion.

36 https://www.eureporter.co/world/russia/2022/03/23/russian-oligarch-who-makes-drone-bombers-to-destroy-ukraine-still-not-sanctioned/.

37 Ibid.
38 https://www.hsgac.senate.gov/wp-content/uploads/imo/media/doc/ HSGAC_Finance_Report_FINAL.pdf.
39 https://en.wikipedia.org/wiki/John_Beyrle.
40 https://en.wikipedia.org/wiki/Solntsevskaya_Bratva.
41 See https://wikileaks.org/plusd/cables/10MOSCOW317_a.html and http://www.cnn.com/2010/WORLD/europe/12/01/russia .wikileaks.index.html.
42 https://oversight.house.gov/release/comer-oversight-republicans-press -yellen-on-russian-oligarch-tied-to-hunter-biden/.

Chapter 5: Mr. Biden Goes to Romania (and Hunter Tries to Free a Corrupt Oligarch)

1 https://oversight.house.gov/wp-content/uploads/2023/05/Bank -Memorandum-5.10.23.pdf.
2 https://nypost.com/2022/08/13/hunter-biden-met-with-dad -immediately-after-romanian-business-meetings/.
3 https://www.the-sun.com/news/3036591/hunter-biden-leverage -obama-romanian-tycoon-avoid-jail/.
4 https://www.nationalreview.com/2023/07/the-biden-familys-history -of-influence-peddling-explained/.
5 https://www.dailymail.co.uk/news/article-12070145/How-Biden -called-corruption-cancer-family-received-1million-payments -tycoon.html.
6 Ibid.
7 Ibid.
8 Ibid.
9 https://www.politico.eu/article/the-dna-of-romanias-anti-corruption -success-eu-transparency-international/.
10 https://www.dailymail.co.uk/news/article-12070145/How-Biden -called-corruption-cancer-family-received-1million-payments -tycoon.html.
11 https://nypost.com/2021/05/20/ex-fbi-chief-gave-100k-to-biden -grandkid-trust-as-he-sought-future-work-hunter-emails/.

12 Ibid.

13 https://www.dailymail.co.uk/news/article-9646127/Hunter-Biden
    -hired-Romanian-tycoon-help-overturn-bribery-conviction.html.

14 https://www.dailymail.co.uk/news/article-12070145/How-Biden
    -called-corruption-cancer-family-received-1million-payments
    -tycoon.html.

15 https://freebeacon.com/biden-administration/hunter-biden-lobbied
    -state-department-in-2016-on-behalf-of-corrupt-romanian-national
    -records-show/.

16 https://en.wikipedia.org/wiki/Nicolae_Ceau%C5%9Fescu.

17 https://www.theguardian.com/world/2019/dec/15/romania
    -orphanage-child-abusers-may-face-justice-30-years-on.

18 https://balkaninsight.com/2016/11/25/romanian-clinics-probe
    -puts-organ-trafficking-in-spotlight-11-24-2016/#:~:text=Organ
    %20trafficking%20has%20been%20an,clinic%20for%20years
    %20until%202013.

Chapter 6: Mr. Biden Goes to Kazakhstan

1 https://www.dailymail.co.uk/news/article-8849097/As-GUY
   -ADAMS-uncovers-links-suspect-regime-just-damage-Hunter
   -Biden-cause.html.

2 Ibid.

3 Ibid.

4 Ibid.

5 Ibid.

6 Ibid.

7 Ibid.

8 Ibid.

9 Ibid.

10 Ibid.

11 Ibid.

12 Ibid.

13 Ibid.

14 Ibid.

Chapter 7: Mr. Biden Goes to California, Gets Someone Killed, and Gets Away with It

1 Schweizer, *Profiles in Corruption*, 77.
2 Ibid., 77.
3 Ibid., 77.
4 Ibid., 78.
5 Ibid., 78.
6 Ibid., 78.

Chapter 8: Mr. Biden Goes to Costa Rica

1 https://qcostarica.com/joe-bidens-brother-frank-linked-to-real-estate-project-in-costa-rica/.
2 https://www.imdb.com/title/tt0031060/characters/nm0000050.
3 Schweizer, *Profiles in Corruption*, 83.

Chapter 9: Mr. Biden Goes to Florida

1 https://abcnews.go.com/Politics/frank-biden-leveraged-famous-business-gain/story?id=68202529.
2 Ibid.
3 Ibid.
4 Ibid.
5 Ibid.
6 Ibid.
7 Ibid.
8 Schweizer, *Profiles in Corruption*, 86.
9 Ibid., 86.
10 Ibid., 87.
11 Ibid., 87.
12 Ibid., 86.
13 Ibid., 89.

Chapter 10: Mr. Biden Goes to Iraq

1 https://www.google.com/search?client=safari&rls=en&sxsrf=APwXEdfkS8LccNC2wmF0WTPTS6HZonHbFQ:16842

66568626&q=hemorrhaging&spell=1&sa=X&ved=2ahUKE
wjzpZ70zfr-AhXhfDABHW0sBfAQkeECKAB6BAgIEAE.

Chapter 11: Mr. Biden Goes off the Reservation

1 Schweizer, *Profiles in Corruption*, 66.

Chapter 12: Ms. Biden Goes to Washington

1 https://nypost.com/2022/04/07/joe-bidens-sister-out-with-memoir
-in-familys-latest-bid-to-profit-off-presidency/ and https://www
.washingtontimes.com/news/2008/oct/15/biden-routes-campaign
-cash-to-family-their-firms/kets.

2 https://nypost.com/2022/04/07/joe-bidens-sister-out-with-memoir
-in-familys-latest-bid-to-profit-off-presidency/.

Chapter 13: Mr. Biden Goes to the IRS

1 https://www.nbcnews.com/politics/justice-department/federal
-prosecutors-hunter-biden-taxes-gun-charge-rcna80692.

2 Schweizer, *Profiles in Corruption*, 66; https://www.nbcnews.com/
politics/politics-news/irs-agent-wants-whistleblower-protections
-discuss-hunter-biden-probe-rcna80564.

3 https://www.washingtonpost.com/national-security/2022/10/06/
hunter-biden-tax-gun-charges/.

4 Schweizer, *Profiles in Corruption*, 66; https://www.nbcnews.com/
politics/joe-biden/hunter-biden-asks-criminal-probe-trump-allies
-laptop-rcna68703.

5 https://www.nbcnews.com/politics/justice-department/
federal-prosecutors-hunter-biden-taxes-gun-charge-rcna
80692.

6 https://sports.yahoo.com/irs-whistleblower-alleges-removal-entire
-135203018.html.

7 Ibid.

8 Ibid.

9 https://www.nationalreview.com/news/way-outside-the-norm-irs
-whistleblower-accuses-agency-of-slow-walking-hunter-biden

-probe/#:~:text="There%20were%20multiple%20steps%20that,deviations%20from%20the%20normal%20process.

Chapter 14: Will Mr. Biden Go to Jail?

1 https://www.oge.gov/web/oge.nsf/Resources/18+U.S.C.+§+208:+Acts+affecting+a+personal+financial+interest.

Chapter 15: Biden Lets China Off the Hook for COVID-19

1 https://2017-2021.state.gov/fact-sheet-activity-at-the-wuhan-institute-of-virology/.
2 https://oversight.house.gov/release/covid-origins-part-2-hearing-wrap-up-intelligence-community-officials-provide-further-evidence-that-covid-19-originated-in-a-wuhan-lab/.
3 Ibid.
4 https://www.reuters.com/business/healthcare-pharmaceuticals/who-advisors-urge-china-release-all-covid-related-data-after-new-research-2023-03-18/.
5 https://www.washingtonpost.com/politics/2021/10/29/repeated-claim-that-fauci-lied-congress-about-gain-of-function-research/.
6 https://www.washingtonpost.com/politics/2023/03/16/lab-leak-theory-polling/.
7 https://www.whitehouse.gov/briefing-room/statements-releases/2021/05/26/statement-by-president-joe-biden-on-the-investigation-into-the-origins-of-covid-19/.
8 https://www.theguardian.com/us-news/2023/mar/01/covid-lab-leak-china-us-relations-biden-administration.
9 See https://www.foxnews.com/politics/white-house-still-backs-gain-function-research-prevent-future-pandemics and https://www.nationalreview.com/news/biden-still-supports-gain-of-function-research-despite-potential-covid-links/.
10 https://www.statnews.com/2023/01/27/federal-panel-approves-plans-to-improve-biosecurity-of-lab-made-virus-research/.
11 Ibid.
12 Ibid.

Chapter 16: Dismantling the Dollar, BRICS by BRICS

1 https://fiscaldata.treasury.gov/americas-finance-guide/national
-deficit/.

2 https://medium.com/the-worlds-economy-and-the-economys
-world/a-short-history-of-americas-economy-since-world-war-ii
-37293cdb640#:~:text=At%20the%20end%20of%20World,net
%20exporter%20of%20petroleum%20products.

3 https://www.imf.org/external/datamapper/PPPSH@WEO/EU/
CHN/USA.

4 https://en.wikipedia.org/wiki/Bretton_Woods_system#:~:text=
Bretton%20Woods%20established%20a%20system,every%20other
%20currency%20was%20pegged.

5 https://www.in2013dollars.com/us/inflation/2017?amount=1.

6 https://www.theepochtimes.com/opinion/why-the-debate-over-the
-debt-ceiling-is-critical-5271989.

7 Ibid.

8 https://www.state.gov/ukraine-and-russia-sanctions/.

9 https://en.wikipedia.org/wiki/BRICS.

10 https://www.imf.org/external/datamapper/PPPSH@WEO/EU/
CHN/USA.

11 https://www.japantimes.co.jp/news/2023/05/25/world/politics
-diplomacy-world/brics-expansion-emerging-economies-join/.

12 https://www.cnn.com/2023/03/31/middleeast/saudi-china-get-closer
-mime-intl/index.html.

13 Ibid.

14 https://foreignpolicy.com/2023/04/24/brics-currency-end-dollar
-dominance-united-states-russia-china/.

15 https://tfiglobalnews.com/2022/08/12/biden-hatches-a
-plan-to-kill-brics-with-sco-a-geopolitical-joke-of-the-funniest
-kind/.

16 Ibid.

17 https://www.breitbart.com/europe/2023/05/31/eu-commission-hails
-end-of-petrodollar-.

18 Ibid.

19 https://events.fitchratings.com/insidetheratingsussovereigndow#:~:text
    =Inside%20the%20Ratings%3A%20US%20Sovereign%20Downgrade
    %20and%20Economic%20Outlook&text=ALREADY%20
    REGISTERED%3F,and%20a%20Stable%20Outlook%20assigned.

Chapter 17: Research and Development China Style—Steal It

1 Navarro and Autry, *Death by China*, 81.
2 Ibid.
3 Ibid.
4 Ibid.
5 John F. Kennedy's inaugural address, https://www.archives.gov/
   milestone-documents/president-john-f-kennedys-inaugural-address.
6 https://www.wsj.com/articles/
   SB10001424052748704814204575507353221141616.
7 Navarro and Autry, *Death by China*, 86.

Chapter 18: Biden Strangles the US Patent Protections

1 http://www.allgov.com/news/top-stories/director-of-the-united
   -states-patent-and-trademark-office-who-is-andrei-iancu-180326
   ?news=860440.
2 https://www.newsweek.com/big-tech-abusing-us-patent-system
   -time-congress-step-opinion-1819256.
3 https://www.uspto.gov/sites/default/files/aia_implementation/
   20110916-pub-l112-29.pdf.
4 https://hbr.org/2022/08/big-tech-has-a-patent-violation-problem
   and https://www.heritage.org/technology/report/big-techs-abuse
   -patent-owners-the-ptab-must-end.
5 https://today.westlaw.com/Document/
   I454ef9f1bc9311ebbea4f0dc9fb69570/View/FullText.html
   ?transitionType=Default&contextData=(sc.Default)&firstPage=true
   and https://www.law360.com/articles/1347266/iancu-leaves-pro
   -patentee-legacy-as-uspto-director.
6 https://www.reuters.com/legal/litigation/biden-administration
   -scraps-policy-tech-standard-patents-2022-06-09/.

7 See https://www.wicker.senate.gov/2022/12/wicker-big-tech-to-face
-renewed-scrutiny-from-congress and https://nypost.com/2022/03/
18/how-big-tech-media-and-dems-killed-the-hunter-biden-story/.

Chapter 19: China Steals Our Inventions

1 https://www.bloomberg.com/news/features/2022-09-15/china
-wanted-ge-s-secrets-but-then-their-spy-got-caught.
2 Ibid.
3 https://www.justice.gov/opa/pr/chinese-telecommunications-device
-manufacturer-and-its-us-affiliate-indicted-theft-trade.
4 Ibid.
5 https://www.yahoo.com/video/us-brings-charges-against-chinese
-182813663.html.
6 https://www.justice.gov/opa/pr/chinese-telecommunications-device
-manufacturer-and-its-us-affiliate-indicted-theft-trade.

Chapter 20: China Funds Our Colleges and Universities to Try to Control Them

1 https://foreignaffairs.house.gov/wp-content/uploads/2020/02/CCP
-Threat-of-American-Universities-V3.pdf.
2 Ibid.
3 Ibid.
4 Ibid.
5 https://www.thecollegefix.com/nearly-170m-in-contracts-and-gifts
-flowed-to-u-s-universities-from-china-in-2021/.
6 https://sites.ed.gov/foreigngifts/.
7 Ibid.
8 Navarro and Autry, *Death by China*, 258.

Chapter 21: China Uses Students to Spy on US Defense Industries

1 https://www.cnn.com/2019/02/01/politics/us-intelligence-chinese
-student-espionage/index.html.
2 Ibid.

3   Ibid.
4   Ibid.
5   Ibid.
6   Ibid.
7   Ibid.
8   Ibid.
9   Ibid.
10   Ibid.
11   Ibid.
12   Ibid.
13   Ibid.

Chapter 22: Biden Abolishes the Program to Fight Chinese Espionage

1   https://www.politico.com/news/2022/02/23/doj-shuts-down-china
     -focused-anti-espionage-program-00011065.
2   Ibid.
3   Ibid.
4   Ibid.
5   https://freebeacon.com/national-security/white-house-fights-to-strip
     -tough-on-china-provisions-from-annual-defense-spending-bill/.
6   Ibid.
7   Ibid.

Chapter 23: Biden Lets Fentanyl from China Flow across Our Borders

1   https://freebeacon.com/national-security/white-house-fights-to-strip
     -tough-on-china-provisions-from-annual-defense-spending-bill/.
2   Ibid.
3   Ibid.

Chapter 24: China Develops a Monopoly of Rare Earth Minerals

1   https://www.reuters.com/markets/commodities/chinas-shrewd
     -grab-green-energy-recycling-dominance-2023-08-18/#:~:text=

China%20has%20been%20the%20clear,energy%20producer%2C
%20according%20to%20Ember.

2   https://www.fpri.org/article/2022/03/chinas-rare-earth-metals
-consolidation-and-market-power/.

3   https://www.usgs.gov/.

4   https://www.whitehouse.gov/briefing-room/statements-releases/
2023/02/15/fact-sheet-biden-harris-administration-announces-new
-standards-and-major-progress-for-a-made-in-america-national
-network-of-electric-vehicle-chargers/#:~:text=To%20ensure
%20ready%20access%20to,500%2C000%20EV%20chargers%20by
%202030.

Chapter 25: Biden Gives Away Our Rare Earth Mineral Mining to Save a Lake

1   https://www.fpri.org/article/2022/03/chinas-rare-earth-metals
-consolidation-and-market-power/.

2   https://www.thecentersquare.com/minnesota/article_10ad5904
-a0b4-11ed-8d13-eb9262030cbc.html#:~:text=(The%20Center
%20Square)%20-%20President,for%20more%20than%2020
%20years.

3   Ibid.

4   Ibid.

Chapter 26: Biden Gives Away Our Oil to China

1   https://nypost.com/2023/08/04/bidens-energy-secretary-called
-china-before-us-tapped-oil-reserves/.

Chapter 27: Biden Helps China's Mind-Control Projects

1   https://www.worldometers.info/world-population/china-population/.

2   https://apnews.com/article/smartphones-business-china-asia-pacific
-us-news-7a01cf8cf13f7681df62094f27b1bcbc.

3   Ibid.

Notes

Chapter 28: Biden Lets China off the Green Hook

1 https://www.carbonbrief.org/analysis-contradictory-coal-data-clouds-chinas-co2-emissions-rebound-in-2022/.

Chapter 29: Biden Lets China Circle the Globe

1 https://www.fpri.org/article/2022/03/chinas-rare-earth-metals-consolidation-and-market-power/.
2 https://thediplomat.com/2014/10/japan-caves-to-china-on-senkaku-island-dispute/.
3 https://www.fpri.org/article/2022/03/chinas-rare-earth-metals-consolidation-and-market-power/.
4 https://www.orfonline.org/expert-speak/chinas-scramble-for-africas-rare-earth-elements/.
5 Ibid.
6 Ibid.
7 https://www.bbc.com/news/world-africa-45809810.
8 https://www.barrons.com/news/controversial-s-leone-radio-interview-with-us-envoy-airs-82e9d168.
9 https://www.thesierraleonetelegraph.com/pressure-mounts-on-illegitimate-president-bio-as-us-envoy-condemns-planned-electoral-review/.
10 https://www.orfonline.org/expert-speak/chinas-scramble-for-africas-rare-earth-elements/.
11 https://fortune.com/2023/05/18/china-belt-road-loans-pakistan-sri-lanka-africa-collapse-economic-instability/.
12 Ibid.
13 Ibid.
14 https://www.theguardian.com/environment/2021/aug/20/water-protests-in-pakistan-erupt-against-chinas-belt-and-road-plan.
15 https://fortune.com/2023/05/18/china-belt-road-loans-pakistan-sri-lanka-africa-collapse-economic-instability/.
16 Ibid.
17 Ibid.

Chapter 30: China Puts a Military Base in Cuba, and Biden Lets Them Do It

1 https://www.wsj.com/articles/beijing-plans-a-new-training-facility
-in-cuba-raising-prospect-of-chinese-troops-on-americas-doorstep
-e17fd5d1.

2 https://www.agenzianova.com/en/news/la-cina-pianifica-costruzione
-di-una-rete-di-cinque-basi-militari-estero/.

Chapter 31: China Uses Belt and Road Initiative to Build Military Bases

1 https://en.wikipedia.org/wiki/Belt_and_Road_Initiative.

2 https://www.washingtonpost.com/national-security/2023/04/26/
chinese-military-base-uae/.

3 Ibid.

4 https://www.whitehouse.gov/build-back-better/.

5 https://www.whitehouse.gov/briefing-room/statements-releases/
2023/05/20/fact-sheet-partnership-for-global-infrastructure-and
-investment-at-the-g7-summit/.

Chapter 32: China's Military Challenge

1 https://en.wikipedia.org/wiki/List_of_countries_by_military
_expenditures.

2 https://www.gisreportsonline.com/r/china-indo-pacific-military/.

3 Ibid.

4 https://freebeacon.com/national-security/sinking-our-future
-bidens-budget-cuts-funds-to-u-s-navy-as-china-ramps-up
-shipbuilding/.

5 Ibid.

6 https://www.wsj.com/articles/ukraine-war-depleting-u-s
-ammunition-stockpiles-sparking-pentagon-concern-11661792188.

7 Ibid.

8 Ibid.

9 Ibid.

10 Ibid.

11 https://www.defensenews.com/pentagon/2022/07/19/the-clutch
-isnt-engaged-yet-lockheed-martin-reports-lower-sales-but-says-it
-expects-growing-demand/.

12 https://www.wsj.com/articles/ukraine-war-depleting-u-s
-ammunition-stockpiles-sparking-pentagon-concern-11661792188.

13 https://foreignpolicy.com/2023/07/05/taliban-afghanistan-arms
-dealers-weapons-sales-terrorism/.

14 https://www.hsgac.senate.gov/wp-content/uploads/imo/media/doc/
HSGAC_Finance_Report_FINAL.pdf.

Chapter 33: China's New Weapons

1 https://www.dia.mil/Portals/27/Documents/News/Military
%20Power%20Publications/China_Military_Power_FINAL_5MB
_20190103.pdf.

2 https://www.businessinsider.com/chinas-showing-off-new-weapons
-likely-to-send-a-message-2019-1#4-super-soldiers-armed-with
-guns-that-shoot-around-corners-4.

3 Ibid.

4 Ibid.

5 Ibid.

6 Ibid.

7 https://www.globaltimes.cn/content/1167915.shtml.

8 https://www.businessinsider.com/chinas-showing-off-new-weapons
-likely-to-send-a-message-2019-1#6-upgraded-stealth-fighter-6.

9 https://nypost.com/2019/01/16/china-on-verge-of-fielding-worlds
-most-modern-weapon-systems-pentagon.

10 Ibid.

11 https://www.businessinsider.com/chinese-troops-train-for-nuclear
-war-in-mock-icbm-strike-exercise-2019-1.

12 https://www.businessinsider.com/chinas-showing-off-new-weapons
-likely-to-send-a-message-2019-1.

Chapter 34: China's Space Race

1 https://www.businessinsider.com/chinese-troops-train-for-nuclear
-war-in-mock-icbm-strike-exercise-2019-1.
2 https://theconversation.com/is-the-us-in-a-space-race-against-china
-203473.
3 https://www.voanews.com/a/china-has-capability-to-use-space-for
-military-purposes-experts-say/6512155.html.
4 Ibid.

Chapter 35: The Unkept Promise

1 https://itif.org/publications/2021/07/26/false-promises-ii-continuing
-gap-between-chinas-wto-commitments-and-its/.
2 Ibid.
3 Ibid.
4 Ibid.
5 Ibid.
6 Ibid.
7 Ibid.

Chapter 36: Here's What China Got from the Bidens

1 https://www.instituteforenergyresearch.org/fossil-fuels/gas-and-oil/
175-ways-the-biden-administration-and-democrats-have-made-it
-harder-to-produce-oil-gas/.

Also by Dick Morris

Bum Rap on American Cities: The Real Causes of Urban Decay
Dick Morris's first book on the regional inequality in the
distribution of federal money, way back when he was a liberal

Behind the Oval Office: Winning the Presidency in the Nineties
A political insider memoir of Morris's work with candidate Bill
Clinton and a *New York Times* bestseller

The New Prince: Machiavelli Updated for the Twenty-First Century
The Dick Morris complete guide to politics

Vote.com
Predicted—with surprising accuracy—how the internet would
reshape politics

*Power Plays: Win or Lose, How History's Great Political Leaders
Play the Game*
The five types of "power plays" and political strategies; how history's
great political leaders win, lose, and play the game; and a *New York
Times* bestseller

*Off with Their Heads: Traitors, Crooks and Obstructionists in
American Politics, Media, and Business*
Points an accusing finger at the many ways the public has been lied to,
misled, pickpocketed, and endangered by the liberals and liberal media
narratives of the War on Terror and a *New York Times* bestseller

Rewriting History
A political rebuttal to Hillary Clinton's autobiography, *Living
History*, and a *New York Times* bestseller

Because He Could
A political rebuttal to Bill Clinton's autobiography, *My Life*, and a *New York Times* bestseller

Condi vs. Hillary: The Next Great Presidential Race
Surveys the candidates' strengths and weaknesses of a possible presidential race between Hillary Clinton and Condoleezza Rice and a *New York Times* bestseller

Outrage: How Illegal Immigration, the United Nations, Congressional Ripoffs, Student Loan Overcharges, Tobacco Companies, Trade Protection, and Drug Companies Are Ripping Us Off . . . and What to Do about It
The corruption and abuses of power of both left and right governing elites the mainstream media does not cover and a *New York Times* bestseller

Fleeced: How Barack Obama, Media Mockery of Terrorist Threats, Liberals Who Want to Kill Talk Radio, the Do-Nothing Congress, Companies That Help Iran, and Washington Lobbyists for Foreign Governments Are Scamming Us . . . and What to Do about It
Reveals the hundreds of ways American taxpayers are routinely fleeced and offers practical agendas we all can follow to help turn the tide and a *New York Times* bestseller

Catastrophe: How Obama, Congress, and the Special Interests Are Transforming a Slump into a Crash, Freedom into Socialism, and a Disaster into a Catastrophe . . . and How to Fight Back
A call to stop President Obama's radical agenda and a complicit Congress before it's too late and a *New York Times* bestseller

2010: Take Back America
A political and policy road map for Republicans to take back Congress from the Democrats and a *New York Times* bestseller

Revolt: How to Defeat Obamacare and Repeal His Socialist Programs
A political game plan for congressional Republicans to use their power to repeal President Obama's socialist agenda

Screwed: How Foreign Countries Are Ripping Us Off and Plundering Our Economy and How Our Leaders Help Them Do It
A necessary wake-up call for every concerned citizen, from middle-class workers and Tea Party conservatives to labor leaders and environmentalists who oppose globalism and its negative economic and environmental repercussions, and a *New York Times* bestseller

Here Come the Black Helicopters: UN Global Governance and the Loss of Freedom
The book Dick Morris considers his most important—the brazen and treacherous liberal plan to circumvent our democratic processes by putting ultimate governing power in the hands of unaccountable international organizations

Power Grab: Obama's Dangerous Plan for One-Party Government
Contends that President Obama is at war with the US Constitution and its provisions that provide for checks and balances and embarked on an outrageous and sweeping scheme to decisively and illegally grab power away from Congress, the courts, and the states to appropriate it to himself

Armageddon: How Trump Can Beat Hillary
Lays out a political war plan to victory for Donald J. Trump to beat Hilary Clinton and win the presidency and a *New York Times* bestseller

Rogue Spooks: The Intelligence War on Donald Trump
The first book to expose the phoniness of the Steele dossier and how the intelligence community made the whole thing up to get Trump out of office and a *New York Times* bestseller

Fifty Shades of Politics: Stories and Memories from American and Foreign Campaigns

A political memoir filled with stories of Dick Morris's long career working with political leaders and their winning campaigns around the world

The Return: Trump's Big 2024 Comeback

Lays out Trump's secret plan to return to the Oval Office in 2024 and a *Wall Street Journal* bestseller

About the Author

DICK MORRIS is the host of *Dick Morris Democracy* and a regular commentator on Newsmax TV and contributes columns and articles to Newsmax. One of the most prominent political consultants in the US, he has been called "the most influential private citizen in America" by *Time* magazine and was the chief strategist for Bill Clinton's reelection and now serves as an adviser to former president Donald J. Trump. Morris is the author of ten *New York Times* bestsellers, including *Armageddon: How Trump Can Beat Hillary* and *The Return: Trump's Big 2024 Comeback.*

Every day Morris delivers his "Lunch Alert!" videos, which are commentaries about the day's news. To subscribe and receive updates on the ongoing investigations into the Biden family's dark money and corruption, go to dickmorris.com.